REFERENCE GUIDE
TO
CASINO GAMBLING
• *HOW TO WIN* •

BY
HENRY J. TAMBURIN

Research Services Unlimited
Casino Gambling Book Publishers
P.O. Box 19727
Greensboro, NC 27419

795
TAM

REFERENCE GUIDE TO CASINO GAMBLING
Copyright©1996 by Henry Tamburin

Address all inquiries to the publisher:
Research Services Unlimited, P.O. Box 19727, Greensboro, NC 27419

Manufactured in the United States of America

Cover design by Ben Jordan
Typeset by Chris Schneider

Second Edition, August 1996
ISBN: 0-912177-12-8
Library of Congress Catalog Card Number: 96-92405

Publisher's Cataloging in Publication
(Prepared by Quality Books, Inc.)

Tamburin, Henry J., 1994-
    Reference guide to casino gambling : how to win / by Henry Tamburin. -- 2nd ed.
    p. cm.
    Includes bibliographical references and index.
    ISBN 0-912177-12-8

    1. Gambling.   I. Title. II. Title: Casino gambling. III. Title: How to win.

GV1301.T35 1996   795
                         QBI96-40051

The material contained in this book is intended to inform and educate the reader and in no way represents an inducement to gamble legally or illegally.

PREFACE

A lot has happened in the casino industry since the first edition of this book 3 years ago. Legalized casino gambling continues to grow with Americans taking 15 million trips to casinos in 1995 (that's only 1 million less than the number who visited amusement parks). The number of different types of casino games has also increased. Therefore, the second edition was expanded to include 9 new games and the rest of the material was updated.

The purpose of the book remains the same. A concise, non-technical beginner's guide that covers the basic playing rules for each game with tips on how to increase your chances of winning.

As I stated in the first edition, I honestly believe that anyone who wants to risk their money in a casino should first read this book. If you do, you will join the ranks of the smart players who not only know how to play, but more importantly, how to win.

TABLE OF CONTENTS

1

THE BASICS

You are in the minority compared to other casino players. Why? The fact that you are reading this book indicates you want to learn how to become a better player. Congratulations! Your efforts will be rewarded.

Let's be honest. Nobody goes to a casino wanting to lose. Even though it's possible to win, for the majority of players it isn't very probable. The reason is that most players do not really understand the games they play and have never prepared a strategy. You'll be different - you will develop that plan - of where to play, how to play, and most importantly, when to quit.

There are, unfortunately, a lot of misconceptions when it comes to casino gambling. What follows are facts - things you need to understand right off the bat, to get you started on the road to becoming a knowledgeable player.

Develop a Plan

Most individuals save their money and spend a lot of time preparing a trip to their favorite casino. But when it comes to spending some time to develop a plan for how they are going to play once they get there is often neglected. You need to decide which games you want to play. Then study and understand how best to play them to give yourself a fighting chance. Setting a strategy - a game plan - long before you enter the casino is an essential part of becoming a winning player.

The Odds Are Against You

The casinos do not depend upon the luck of their dealers to stay in business. They have the odds in their favor on virtually every bet. But you control the margin of their edge by how well you play. Your goal is to play well enough to cut their edge or casino advantage to less than 1.5%. This is smart casino gambling. The lower the casino's advantage, the greater is your chance of winning something or minimizing your losses.

Don't Drink and Play

There is a reason why alcoholic drinks are free to players. You need to maintain your concentration when you play and drinking alcohol will dull your senses. Better to play sober and do your alcoholic drinking afterwards.

Don't Play with Scared Money

You've heard this before but it's worth repeating. **Gamble with money you can afford to lose should the worst happen.** Using the rent money to gamble in a casino is one of the biggest mistakes anyone can make. Any gambler who does this needs professional help.

Budget Your Money

Always divide your bankroll by the number of playing sessions. If you plan to spend two days gambling figure on two playing sessions per day. If your total bankroll is $500, then allocate one-quarter or $125 to each session. Do not under any circumstances lose more than your allocated $125 per playing session. This is smart management of your gaming bankroll.

Don't Bet More When Losing

When you lose a bet, never increase the size of the next bet to get even. This type of betting, known as the martingale betting progression, can turn into a financial disaster. Avoid this method of betting.

Bet More When Winning

Smart players increase their bets gradually when they are winning. This way it's possible to capitalize on a winning streak should it occur.

Set a Loss Limit

Always set a limit on the amount you are willing to lose and stick to it! If you can't or won't do this, you will never become a successful casino player. **This is the most important fact that you need to practice when you gamble in a casino!**

Take the Profits and Run

One of the advantage we have as players is that we can quit playing anytime we want. When Lady Luck shines on you and the chips are piling up, be prepared to quit when the tide turns. Never lose back your profits - always take them and run!

Set Reasonable Expectations

Sitting down at a blackjack table with $100 and expecting to win $1000 is unrealistic. You will most likely lose your $100 long before you win the $1000. Set reasonable win goals - winning 20-50% of your bankroll is a good rule of thumb.

Look for Values

Just like you go shopping for a car or house to get the best value, you need to do the same in a casino. The casino's edge is not constant for all games. It varies a lot from game to game and even among the different bets in a particular game. You need to understand which bets have value - the ones which have the lowest possible edge - to minimize your losses and maximize your chances of winning more.

Smart casino players also take advantage of special offers from casinos as an inducement to gamble. The most popular is the frequent player clubs where players are issued their own card which they either insert into a card reader when playing the slot machines or hand to a floor person when playing a table game. The casinos will track the amount of time and average bet that a player makes and use this information to reward players with cash, discounted rooms, meals, or show tickets, and more. These casino offers have value and can often either reduce a players overall potential gambling losses or allow a player to eek out a potential profit.

So let's recap. Your goal is to be a smart casino player who knows how to make bets with the lowest casino advantage, understands the principles of sound money management and knows when to take advantage of special casino offers. If you learn and practice these principles, you will have the confidence and skills you need to be a knowledgeable, winning casino player.

2

WHICH GAMES TO PLAY

The casino offers a variety of games to the public. The casino's edge or advantage is different for each game. The higher the casino advantage, the *less* is your chance of winning.

Let's make sure you understand the concept of casino advantage. The latter is sometimes called vigorish or vig. Think of it as a hidden tax.

Let's look at two scenarios, namely, what happens when you lose a bet in a casino, and what happens when you win.

There is no discussion when it comes to losing a bet. When you lose, the bet is lost period.

But what happens when you win? Instead of receiving a fair payout for a winning bet, you are charged a hidden tax. It works like this.

A fair payout, for example, on a winning $1 wager on a number in roulette is $37. When you win, however, the casino only pays you $35. It keeps the $2, like a tax. The $2 sort of disappears into the casino's coiffeurs without you even knowing it!

The irony of all this, is that the casino generates its profits when players win by charging this hidden tax.

What you need to know is how much is this hidden tax and what you can do to reduce it. Because the lower you reduce this tax or casino advantage, the greater will be your chances of winning more or at least minimizing your losses.

The following table summarizes the casino's advantage for different casino games. A positive casino advantage means the casino has the edge. A negative casino advantage implies the player has the better of it. Most casino games have several different types of wagers which is why you see a range of casino advantage for most games.

GAME	CASINO'S ADVANTAGE
Blackjack (without basic strategy)	+5.0% to +10%
Blackjack (with basic strategy)	0 to +0.5%
Blackjack (basic strategy and card count)	−0.2% to -1.0% (player advantage)
Craps	+0.2% to +17%
Pai Gow Poker	−0.2% to +2.5%
Baccarat	+0.1% to +14.1%
Roulette	+2.6% to +7.9%
Big Six Wheel	+11.1% to +22.2%
Video Poker	−0.1% to +5.0%
Red Dog	+3.5%
Sic Bo	+2.8% to +47.5%
Poker	Depends very much on skill level
Slots	+0.5% to +10% or more
Keno	+20% to +50%
Let It Ride	+3.5%
Caribbean Stud Poker	+5.2%

The best games - the ones with the lowest potential casino advantage - are the following casino games:

Blackjack (with at least basic playing strategy)
Craps (but only specific bets)
Baccarat
Video Poker (full pay machines with expert strategy)
Pai Gow Poker
Table Poker (but very dependent upon the skill of fellow players)

These are the casino games which offer you the highest potential of maximizing your winnings or minimizing your losses. They should be a part of every casino players game plan.

3

BLACKJACK

Blackjack is by far the most popular table game in a casino. It is also the very best game from the player's perspective because you can reduce the casino's advantage to 0 or even enjoy a slight edge with skillful play.

Objective

To beat the dealer by either having your cards total higher than the dealer's cards, or the dealer busts (exceeds 21) when the player has 21 or less.

Card Values

The cards from 2 through 10 count face value. All picture cards count ten. The ace counts as 1 or 11 at the player's discretion. Hands which contain an ace counted as 11 are known as soft hands (eg. A, 6 is soft 17). All other hands are known as hard hands (eg. 10, 7 or 10, 6, ace are hard 17 hands).

Mechanics

Every table has a posted minimum and maximum bet. Cash can be exchanged for chips at the table. Casinos use either single or multiple decks of cards. Single and double-deck games are normally dealt by hand with one or both player's cards dealt face down. When four or more decks are used, the player cards are dealt face-up from a dealing shoe. The dealer will have one card face-up and one face-down. The dealers will not reveal their hole or face-down card until all players have completed their hands. The dealers must take an extra card if their cards total 16 or less and continue doing so until the cards total at least 17. When the dealer's cards total 17 thru 21, the dealers must stand and are not permitted to draw an extra card. Some casinos require the dealers to draw if their cards total soft 17. This is not as advantageous to the player as casinos that require the dealers to stand on soft 17.

Player Options

Players communicate their options to the dealer either through hand signals, position of their cards or supplemental bets. The only playing option which you verbally state your intention to the dealer is the surrender option. Keep in mind that for dealer hand held games players are permitted to handle the initial two cards and may use these cards to signal playing options. With multiple games dealt from a dealing shoe all player cards are dealt face up and players are not allowed to handle the cards. Hand signals are used to indicate playing options.

Hit: Request another card. Give a hand signal by either scratching index finger on the table for games in which cards are dealt face-up *or* scratching the cards on the table for cards dealt face-down.

Stand: Satisfied with hand total - no more cards. Give hand signal by waving hand over cards for games in which cards are dealt face-up or tuck the cards under the chips for cards dealt face-down.

Double Down: Double your bet by putting the same (or less) amount of chips next to the original wager. When you double down you will receive *only* one draw card (you can't request more cards). Normally casinos allow players to double down on any two card total. However, there are exceptions and its always **to the player's disadvantage** if the casino restricts the double down option. When you want to double down never add chips on top of your original wager - always place them *next* to the original wager.

Pair Splitting: Any two identical value cards can be split and played as two separate hands. As many additional cards as you wish may be drawn to each split hand except a pair of aces (majority of casinos only allow *one* draw card to each split ace). The signal for pair splitting is to place an amount of chips equal to your original bet *next* to your original bet in the betting area (like doubling down). Some casinos allow a player to resplit a second and even third time if the second card to each split card is identical (i.e. casinos will allow a player to play up to four hands). Likewise, some casinos allow players to double down on each split hand. This is a favorable option to the player when allowed.

Surrender: After receiving the first two cards, a player may surrender. This means giving up one-half of your initial wager and forfeiting the hand. In the majority of casinos that allow surrender, players can only surrender after receiving their initial two cards and prior to requesting any more cards (once you ask for a hit you can't surrender). When a player surrenders they are no longer involved in the round of play. Signal surrender by saying, "surrender."

Insurance: When the dealer has an ace showing (that means face-up) he will ask if the players want to take insurance. A player may make an insurance wager equal to one half of the original bet. You win the insurance bet at a 2 to 1 payoff if the dealer has blackjack. You lose the insurance bet if the dealer does not have a blackjack (i.e. his down card is *not* a ten value card). The insurance wager is placed in a special area of the layout that signifies the insurance bet (just above where players place their wagers). If a player and dealer have a blackjack, most casinos allow the player the option to take even money which is equivalent to insuring the blackjack hand.

Additional Notes
- A blackjack hand consists of an ace and a ten value card (10, J, Q, K). It is a two card 21 and as such will beat three or more card 21's.

- Players will win their wager if their hand totals higher than the dealers. The payoff is 1 to 1. All hands that total less than the dealers will lose. If the player's and dealer's hands total the same, this is a tie (called a push) and no chips are exchanged. The dealer will signal this by tapping the table.

- Never touch your original wager until a decision is rendered for the hand. For games in which the player's cards are dealt face-up, do not touch or handle the cards. Even if you want to pair split, do not handle the cards - the dealer will split the cards.

- When you place your bet, always stack your chips in one neat pile with the higher denomination chips on the bottom of the pile and lower on top. Chips have different colors denoting their denomination. Normally a white chip represents $1, red (or nickel) is $5, yellow is $10, green (or quarter) is $25 and black chips are $100. If you win a hand do not pick up your original wager until after the dealer pays off your win.

- In some casinos the dealers are not permitted to look at their hole card until *after* all players complete their hands. If a player doubles down or pair splits and the dealer ends up with a blackjack, the subsequent bet made by the player is returned to them (only the original wager is lost). In addition, if a player is allowed to surrender prior to the dealer checking his hole card this is known as early surrender as opposed to the regular or late surrender option. Early surrender is a very favorable player option.

New Options and Payoffs

To increase player interest in blackjack, many casinos have recently started to offer new options and special payoffs. These are options and a casino may or may not offer them to the player.

Over-Under 13: This is a side bet that can be made by blackjack players in which they are betting that the total of their first two cards is either greater than or less than 13. For example, if you bet under 13 and your first two cards total 2 thru 12, you win your bet (1 to 1 payoff). If your cards total 13 or higher, you lose the bet. Same rules for the over 13 bet except you are betting that the first two cards total over 13. The ace always counts as one. Once the over/under bet is settled, the twenty one hand is played out. The casino's advantage for the under 13 bet is about 10% and for the over 13 bet, 6.5%.

Multiple Action Blackjack: This new blackjack game was created by the Four Queens Casino in downtown Las Vegas and is being licensed by them to other casinos. This game allows players to make three separate wagers on the same hand. After the dealers complete their hand for the first wager, the dealers keep their upcard and complete a second hand against the players original hand. This is repeated a third time to determine the outcome of the third hand. Thus the players hand is used for three games in which the dealer's upcard remains constant.

Most players will not hit a 12 through 16 hand for fear of busting and automatically losing 3 bets. This is a big mistake. If you play Multiple Action Blackjack, you need to use the same basic playing strategy as the regular game.

Double Exposure Blackjack: This is another unique variation of blackjack in which both dealer cards are dealt face-up. However, because you can see both of the dealer's cards, the playing rules are modified. This includes paying blackjacks at 1 to 1 (except the A, J of diamonds is paid at 2 to 1), doubling down is only permitted on hands that total 9, 10, or 11 (doubling on soft hands is not permitted), surrender, insurance and resplits are not allowed and all tie hands result in a loss (except a player's blackjack beats a dealer's blackjack). Because of these rule changes, double exposure blackjack is not as favorable a game as the normal casino blackjack game.

Five Card 21: Some casinos pay a bonus 2 to 1 payoff, if the player hand totals 21 in five cards.

Six Card Automatic Winner: If a player has six cards that total 21 or less, the hand is an automatic winner.

6,7,8: If a player gets a 21 with a 6,7,8 of the same suit, the player receives a 2 to 1 bonus payoff.

7,7,7: If a player gets a three card 7 hand (totaling 21), the player receives a 3 to 2 bonus payoff.

Red or Black: You wager on the color of the dealer's up-card. If you guess right you are paid even money. If the up-card is a deuce of the color you selected, this is a push or tie (you don't win or lose). This gives the casino a 3.8% advantage.

Super 7's: Players can make an optional side bet that wins if a player's hand contains one or more 7's. If one of the first two player cards contain a 7, the player receives a 3 to 1 payoff. If the first two player cards are a pair of 7's, the player wins more (suited wins more than unsuited). And if the player receives a third 7, the payoffs are up to $5,000 (suited).

Royal Match: Players make an optional side bet on whether the first two cards will be suited. The payoff varies depending upon the number of decks. For example, in an eight deck game, the payoff is 2 to 1. If the first two player cards are a king and queen of same suit, this is known as a royal match and the payoff is typically 25 to 1.

21 Super Bucks: Players make an optional side bet on a progressive jackpot. Extra payouts occur if a player receives any of the following hands: blackjack (2 to 1); any pair of tens or more (3 to 1); any suited blackjack (10 to 1); ace and jack suited (50 to 1); 4, 5, 6 suited on first three cards (500 to 1); 2, 3, 4, 5 on first four cards (5,000 to 1 or 10% of progressive jackpot); and suited ace, 2, 3, 4, 5 on first five cards wins the entire progressive jackpot.

Heads Up: This variation is in its infancy. It's a fast version of blackjack in which all players at a table play the same two community cards. Each player makes his/her own decision on how to play the hand based on dealer's upcard. Thus if the community cards were a 10 and 5, player #1 may stand, player #2 may hit, and so forth.

Progressive Blackjack: This relatively new game offers the player an optional side bet with a progressive jackpot and is based on the player being dealt aces. In fact the more aces, the more money you can win. If the first two player cards are aces, the player receives $25. If the aces are suited, the progressive payoff increases to $100. If you split aces and draw a third ace, the payoff is $250. If the three aces are of the same suit, the bonus increases to $2,500. Get four aces in a row of the same color (either four hearts and diamonds *or* four spades and clubs) and the player wins the total on the progressive jackpot meter. Atlantic City casinos, for example, start the jackpot at $50,000 and 70 cents of every dollar wagered on the progressive bet is added to the jackpot.

Spanish 21: This is a modified version of blackjack with rule variations and plenty of bonuses. The game is dealt with 6 decks of cards in which all the 10's have been removed. This leads to fewer blackjack hands and less dealer breaking.

The playing rules include:
- Insurance
- Late surrender
- Player blackjack beats dealer blackjack and pays 3 to 2
- Player total of 21 beats dealer total of 21 and pays 1 to 1
- Player may resplit pairs including aces up to three times
- Player may double down on any number of cards including after pair splitting
- Player may double down for less
- Player may "rescue" or take back the doubled portion of a non-busted double down hand and forfeit the original wager (this rule is known as the double down rescue)

The payoffs and bonuses include:
Blackjack paid at 3 to 2
Five card 21 paid at 3 to 2
Six card 21 paid at 2 to 1
Seven card 21 paid at 3 to 1
6-7-8 suited paid at 2 to 1
6-7-8 spades paid at 3 to 1
6-7-8 mixed paid at 3 to 2
7-7-7 suited paid at 2 to 1 (possible jackpot)
7-7-7 spades paid at 3 to 1
7-7-7 mixed paid at 3 to 2

The basic playing strategy for Spanish 21 is complicated (See Appendix 1). Even using it, the casino's edge is still slightly higher than the regular game of blackjack.

Of all the above new options, the best for the basic strategy player is the 2 to 1 payoff for the five card 21. The options with the greatest profit potential for someone who is keeping track of the cards as they are played (more about this later), is the over/under 13 bet and the progressive side bet on aces in Progressive Blackjack.

New Procedures
Two new devices have found their way on blackjack tables.

Maxtime: This is a new dealing procedure that is becoming very popular. A flashlight type device is built into the blackjack table in front of the dealer. Whenever the dealer has a ten (or ace) up-card, the dealer will slide the cards over this device and through a small window he can see the corner of the hole card. Dealers can see if they have an ace (or ten) hole card and thus a natural without peeking at the down-card. This device eliminates any chance of a player sneaking a peek at the dealer's hole card.

Shufflemaster: This is an automatic shuffling device that has found wide acceptance in casinos. While the dealers are dealing the cards from one (or more) decks, the shufflemaster is automatically shuffling the second deck(s). With the shufflemaster, casinos do not have to spend a lot of wasted time manually shuffling cards between one shoe and the next. From their perspective, time is money.

Recommendation
Blackjack is your best bet in the casino but to consistently win you must learn to play with favorable rules and learn the correct basic playing strategies. These computer derived strategies will nearly eliminate the casinos normal 5 to 10% advantage over the unskilled players. Once you have mastered the basic strategy, the serious player who wants to get the edge over the casino should learn the optimum strategy known as card counting.

Effects of Rule Changes
The following information can be used to estimate the effects various rules have on the casino's advantage. Numbers with a positive sign indicate the percent advantage to the casino. Numbers with a negative sign are player favorable rules.

Single deck	No Advantage
Two decks	+0.35%
Four decks	+0.52%
Six decks	+0.58%
Eight decks	+0.61%
Dealer hits soft 17	+0.20%
Double on 9, 10 and 11 only	+0.10%
Double on 10 or 11 only	+0.20%
Resplit aces	−0.05%
Double down after splitting	−0.13%
Late surrender	−0.05%
Early surrender	−0.62%
No splitting of aces	+0.17%
Double on 3 or more cards	−0.21%
Six card automatic winner	−0.15%
Natural pays 2 to 1	+2.30%

Using the above information it is possible to estimate the casino's advantage for any given set of rules. For example a two deck game in which the dealer stands on soft 17 and the casino allows doubling after pair splitting would have an estimated casino advantage of +0.22%.

Two deck game	+0.35%
Double down after pair splitting	-0.13%
Casino Advantage	+0.22%

Recommendation

Your best game is a single deck game vs. a multiple deck game. The more decks the casinos use, for the same set of rules, the greater is their advantage. The very best games for the most commonly offered options are when the dealer must stand on soft 17, there are no restrictions on doubling down, the latter is permitted after pair splitting and the surrender option. *To be a consistent winner, play only those games with the most favorable playing rules.*

Basic Playing Strategy

As mentioned previously, the casino's edge over an unskilled blackjack player is about 5%. You can lower this edge significantly by learning a computer derived strategy known as the basic playing strategy.

A casual player can reduce the casino's edge to about 1% by learning the following 9 rules.

Simplified Blackjack Playing Strategy

Your Hand	Playing Strategy vs. Dealer's Upcard
12 thru 16	Stand on 2 thru 6, hit on 7 thru ace
17 thru 21	Stand
10 or 11	Double on 2 thru 9
Soft 13 thru 17	Always hit except double on 5,6
Soft 18 thru 21	Always stand except double soft 18 on 5,6
8,8 and ace,ace	Always split
2,2; 3,3; 6,6; 7,7; 9,9	Split on 2 thru 7 (except stand on 9,9 vs 7)
5,5: 10,10	Never split

NEVER TAKE INSURANCE

You should not play blackjack in a casino until you at least mastered the above condensed basic strategy. Better yet, learn the complete basic strategy summarized in the next section.

Multiple Deck Basic Strategy

The following table summarizes the computer derived playing strategy which covers every playing decision a player normally makes. The table is the specific basic strategy for multiple decks and dealer standing on soft 17. Basic strategy for different rules and number of decks is contained in Appendix I.

The playing strategy is based on your hand and the value of the dealer's upcard. For example, if you were dealt a 7,4 (11) the table below states to double down if dealer upcard is any value from 2 to 10. If instead, the dealer upcard is an ace, then you should hit the 11. Likewise, the table indicates that if you were dealt a pair of 2's, you should split if the dealer upcard is 2, 3, 4, 5, 6, 7. If the dealer upcard is any other card, then you should hit ("otherwise hit").

Multiple Deck Basic Strategy
Double-down on any two cards
Double-down after pair splitting

Your Hand	Playing Strategy vs. Dealer's Upcard
5 to 8	Always Hit.
9	Double on 3 to 6, otherwise hit.
10	Double on 2 to 9, hit on 10,A.
11	Double on 2 to 10, hit on A.
12	Stand on 4 to 6, otherwise hit.
13	Stand on 2 to 6, otherwise hit.
14	Stand on 2 to 6, otherwise hit.
15	Stand on 2 to 6, otherwise hit.
16	Stand on 2 to 6, otherwise hit.
17	Always stand.
18	Always stand.
A,2	Double on 5, 6, otherwise hit.
A,3	Double on 5, 6, otherwise hit.
A,4	Double on 4 to 6, otherwise hit.
A,5	Double on 4 to 6, otherwise hit.
A,6	Double on 3 to 6, otherwise hit.
A,7	Double on 3 to 6. Stand on 2, 7 or 8. Hit on 9, 10 or A.
A,8 to A,10	Always stand.
A,A	Always split.
2,2	Split on 2 to 7, otherwise hit.
3,3	Split on 2 to 7, otherwise hit.
4,4	Split on 5, 6, otherwise hit.

5,5 . . . . Never split. Treat as 10.
6,6 . . . . Split on 2 to 6, otherwise hit.
7,7 . . . . Split on 2 to 7, otherwise hit.
8,8 . . . . Always split.
9,9 . . . . Split on 2 to 6, 8 or 9.
Stand on 7, 10, or A.
10,10 . . . . Always stand.

This previous multiple deck basic strategy is valid if the players are allowed to double down after pair splitting. If doubling down is *not* allowed after pair splitting, then use the following pair splitting rules.

| | **Playing Strategy vs.** |
| **Your Hand** | **Dealer's Upcard** |

2,2 . . . . Split on 4 to 7, otherwise hit.
3,3 . . . . Split on 4 to 7, otherwise hit.
4,4 . . . . Never split, always hit.
6,6 . . . . Split on 3 to 6, otherwise hit.

Recommendation

It is imperative to learn and use this basic strategy. The easiest way to do this is make up flash cards using index cards and put the dealer's upcard and player's hand on one side and the correct strategy on the other side. Flip through your flash cards until you can remember each decision without error. One more note: Do not under any circumstances make the insurance bet (or take even money) even if you are dealt a blackjack. The casino's advantage is too high (about 6 to 8%). *Never, never take insurance.*

Card Counting

Blackjack card counters are feared by casinos because they have the edge over them and in the long run will win more money than they lose. This is the reason why casinos sometimes bar card counters from playing blackjack. But don't let this stop you from learning this optimum playing strategy. By properly disguising your skills you can card count without fear of being barred.

Learning to count cards is not something you do in a few hours. It requires time to learn and practice your card counting strategies before risking money in a casino.

It is beyond the scope of this book to dwell in great detail on the technique of card counting. However, I will review the basics of card counting so that you have an understanding of what it is, how to use it, and why it works.

A large number of computer studies that have been done on card counting all confirm the fact that:

- Whenever the remaining ratio of cards left to be dealt contains an abundance of ten value cards, the player has the advantage and should make a larger bet size.

- Whenever the remaining ratio of cards left to be dealt contains an abundance of low value cards (2, 3, 4, 5, 6's), the player is at a disadvantage and should make the minimum bet size.

A card counter keeps track of the ratio of high to low cards by assigning point count values to each card. For example, the low value cards 2, 3, 4, 5, 6 would have a count value of +1. Likewise, the tens, picture cards and aces have the count value of -1. All other cards have a 0 count value.

As the cards are played, the counter arithmetically adds the count value of every card on the table. Thus, if the first player has a 6, 4, 8, the counter's sum is a +2. That's because the 6 and 4 each have a +1 value and the 8 has a 0 count value. Adding the

+1 to the +1 the sum is +2. If the next player shows a Jack and 7, the point value of these cards (which are -1 and 0) must be added to the +2. The net sum is +1 [i.e. +2+(-1)=+1]. In this manner, the counter continues to add the +1's and -1's until the round is completed. When this occurs, the counter has either a plus number or minus number or perhaps 0 as the arithmetic sum. The latter is known as the running count. And if the running count is positive, it means the player has the advantage in the next deal. Likewise, if the running count is negative, the dealer now has the advantage. The more positive the running count, the greater is the player's advantage and the larger should be the bet size.

A suggested bet size based upon the running count is as follows:

Single Deck Game

Running Count	Bet Size
negative to +1	1 unit*
+ 2	2 units
+ 3	3 units
+ 4 or more	4 units

Multiple Deck Game

Running Count	Bet Size
Negative to +3	1 unit
+ 4 to +6	2 units
+ 7 to +9	3 units
+ 10 or more	4 units

If you follow the basic playing strategy and size your bets based upon the running count, you will now join an elite group of skillful casino players that have the advantage over the casino. In

---

*If your minimum bet if $5.00, then $5.00 represents 1 unit, $10.00 would be 2 units, and so forth.

other words, over the long run, you can't lose.

Practice card counting at home by taking a deck of cards and flip them over one at a time. As you see each card, keep the running count. You will know you are keeping an accurate count if your final count after going through the deck of cards totals 0. Keep practicing until you can accurately count down a single deck of cards in about 30 seconds.

There are other refinements to card counting which can be learned once the basics are mastered. These include true count wagering, team play and more. But walk before you run - start first by mastering bet sizing based upon the running count.

Final Tips
1. Shuffle tracking is a new technique being used by skilled players to follow slugs of high or low cards through the shuffle. By knowing where these slugs of cards exist in the multiple decks, a skillfull player can position the cut card to either put these slugs into play or not.

    Here's one way to try this new technique. If you are card counting and you have a positive count just when the cut card comes out of the shoe, then you know the cards left in the shoe must be rich in high cards. If you follow this slug of high cards through the shuffle (this does take practice) and know approximately where these cards are located, you can put the cut card such that this slug of high cards ends up at the top of the stack of cards. This way you'll know the more favorable player cards (high cards) will be dealt at the beginning of the shoe and with this knowledge you can bet more.

    Arnold Snyder, publisher of *Blackjack Forum* newsletter, presented an excellent summary of shuffle tracking in a three part series (see Suggested Reading).

2. If you are card counting, disguise your bet size increases so as not to attract attention. You are better off making two bets of $10 vs. one bet of $20. Above all, do *not* make sudden

increases in your bet size from say 1 to 4 units. Better to gradually increase your bet size (1 to 2 then 4 units) if the count warrants. Also, avoid playing for long periods in negative counts. Stop betting or take a break.

3. Don't offer any advice to other players as to how to play their hand. Likewise be patient if other players give you advice because usually it will be incorrect. This also holds for playing advice given by dealers and floor supervisors.

4. To prevent making mistakes in basic strategy it is helpful to take a hand held basic strategy card with you to the tables. You can refer to this card if you forget how to make the correct play. You should not use this card as a substitute for memorizing the basic strategy.

5. Special card counting techniques can turn a lousy bet such as the under/over 13 or progressive blackjack side bet into a profitable bet. Advanced blackjack books will show you the techniques needed to take advantage of these blackjack side bets (see Suggested Reading).

6. Another way to win money at blackjack is to enter a blackjack tournament. Many casinos offer regularly scheduled weekly "fun" tournaments where the entry fee is relatively low (often less that $50). The objective in blackjack tournaments is to end up with more money (chips) then your fellow players after a specified number of hands. Be careful, however, because money management and sometimes playing strategy is different than the regular game. Before you enter a tournament, I suggest you read one of the excellent texts on tournament gaming.

7. An electronic version of blackjack, known as Live Video Blackjack, has sprung up in casinos. A bank of five player video terminals set in a horseshoe arrangement with a sixth dealer video screen set in the middle facing the players. This

screen shows the dealer's hand and simulates the shuffle and deal of the cards. Players sit at one of the terminals and use push buttons to signal hitting, standing, splitting, doubling and insurance. Players can double down on any two cards but multiple pair splitting and doubling after pair splitting is not allowed.

The advantage of Live Video Blackjack vs. the standard game is the relatively low minimum bets (often $1). However, the computer will always round down for payoffs. If you bet a dollar and get a blackjack you will only be paid a dollar. It's important therefore to always wager an even amount to get the maximum payoff (in the case of a blackjack hand, the payoff would be $3 for every $2 wagered).

Summary

To be a smart blackjack player you must:

1. Select the games with the most favorable rules.
2. Memorize the basic blackjack playing strategy.
3. Learn how to keep track of the cards (card counting) for betting purposes.

"Blackjack is the only casino game an amateur can learn to play and at which he can definitely win."

Lawrence Revere

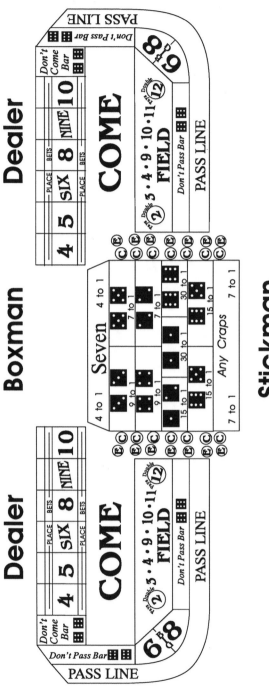

4

CRAPS

Casino craps is the fastest and most exciting game and offers the player several of the best bets in the house. However, most novice players are reluctant to play because they are confused by the multitude of bets on the layout, and the fast action on the table. In fact, the majority of the bets on the layout are "sucker bets" which have a very high casino edge. The key to winning is to confine your play to those 20% wagers with a casino edge of 1.5% or less.

Objective

To correctly predict the outcome of one roll or a series of rolls of the dice.

Dice Probabilities

Everything you need to know about dice probabilities is shown graphically on the next page. It depicts how many different ways you can roll any of the numbers (2 through 12) with a pair of dice. This is summarized on page 31.

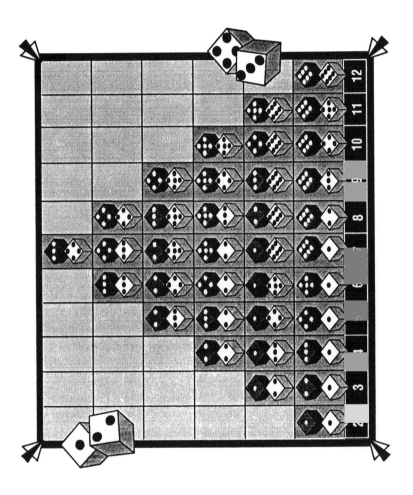

Numbers	Combination	Ways To Make
2	1-1	1
3	1-2, 2-1	2
4	1-3, 3-1, 2-2	3
5	1-4, 4-1, 2-3, 3-2	4
6	1-5, 5-1, 2-4, 4-2, 3-3	5
7	1-6, 6-1, 2-5, 5-2, 3-4, 4-3	6
8	2-6, 6-2, 3-5, 5-3, 4-4	5
9	3-6, 6-3, 4-5, 5-4	4
10	4-6, 6-4, 5-5	3
11	5-6, 6-5	2
12	6-6	1
		36

A quick look at the chart above reveals that a four can be rolled in three different combinations and a seven in six different combinations. Hence the odds of rolling a four before a seven are 6 to 3 or 2 to 1. Using the above, it is easy to calculate the odds of any number being rolled vs a seven or the odds of rolling a number (odds of rolling a seven are 30 to 6 or 5 to 1).

For example, what are the odds of rolling a 6 before a 7? If you check the above chart, you'll see the odds are 6 to 5.

Although you can calculate any odds you want from the above chart, the most important odds for the bets you will be making are the following:

Number	Odds of Making Before the 7
4,10	2 to 1
5,9	3 to 2
6,8	6 to 5

How The Game is Played

There are always at least 4 casino employees who run the

game. The person with the stick controls the pace of the game by moving the dice to players with the stick. Two other dealers take care of paying off winning bets and collecting losing bets on their half of the layout (the crap layout is the same on both ends and is separated in the middle by bets known as proposition bets - see layout p. 28). The casino employee that sits in the middle of the action with the casino bank in front of him/her, is the box person. He/She is the boss of the table and has the final say in event of disputes.

The basics of craps is easy. At the start of a new crap game, one of the players will be offered 5 or so dice by the stick person. The player picks up any two dice and throws them toward the opposite end of the table with enough force so they rebound against the back wall. This first roll has a name. It's called the come out roll. And just prior to the come out roll, all the players around the crap table will be making bets. The most common is a bet on the pass line, which runs all around the outside of the layout.

The rules for winning the pass line bet on the come out roll is as follows:

•You *win* if shooter throws the numbers 7 or 11 (naturals).
•You *lose* if shooter throws the numbers 2, 3, or 12 (crap numbers).

Throw naturals and everyone betting on the pass line wins. Throw craps, and everyone loses.

About a third of the time the shooter will throw either naturals or craps on the come out roll. The other two thirds of the time, he/she will instead throw one of the numbers that appears at the top of the layout (4,5,6,8,9,10).

These numbers are known as point numbers and when a shooter throws one of these numbers on the come out roll, that number becomes the point number. The dealers will in fact mark the point number with a puck (looks like a hockey puck).

When the shooter establishes a point number on the come

out throw, the rules for winning the pass line bets change. Now the shooter is obliged to continue to throw the dice (known as point rolls) until one of two events occur.

> If the shooter repeats the point number before throwing a 7, then all bets on pass line win.

> If instead the shooter throws the 7 before repeating the point number, then all pass line bets lose.

Keep the following in mind.

1. The 7 is a big winner for pass line bettors if it is thrown on the come out roll but if it's thrown on point rolls the 7 makes losers out of pass line bettors.

2. The 2, 3, 12 and 11 only effect a pass line decision on the come out roll. On point rolls, they have no effect on winning or losing the pass line.

In reality, prior to each dice roll, most players will be making other bets on the layout. There are a bunch of them, each with their own win or lose rules. For example, you can make a wager that the very next roll of the dice will be a 7. The shooter throws the 7 on the next dice roll, you win and get paid the listed payoff (4 to 1). If shooter throws any other number, you lose your bet (this is known as a one roll bet).

Your game plan is to make only bets with a maximum casino advantage of 1.5%. This means we will concentrate on the following bets.

Pass Line
Don't Pass Line
Come
Don't Come
Place Bet on 6 and 8
Odds Bet

Before I describe winning techniques for the above bets, let's summarize all the bets on the crap table.

Bets and Payoffs: The following describes the bets available, the rules for winning or losing and the payoffs:

Pass Line: Wins on 7 or 11 on come-out (1st) rolls; loses on 2, 3 or 12. On point rolls, wins if point number (first number rolled, when NOT 2, 3, 7, 11, or 12) is repeated before a 7 and loses if a 7 appears before the point. *Casino Advantage - 1.4%.*

Don't Pass Line: Opposite of pass line. Win on 2, 3 on come-out roll; lose on 7 and 11. On 12 it is a standoff. On point rolls, player wins if 7 appears before point number; loses if point number appears before 7. *Casino Advantage - 1.4%*

Come: Same bet as pass line except this bet is made on point-rolls only. *Casino Advantage - 1.4%*

Don't Come: Same bet as don't pass except this bet is made on point rolls. *Casino Advantage - 1.4%*

Field: One roll wager that can be made before any dice roll. Wins if the next dice roll is 2, 3, 4, 9, 10, 11, 12 and loses if 5, 6, 7, 8 is rolled. Pays 1 to 1 on all winning numbers except 2 or 12. The latter pay either 2 to 1 or 3 to 1. *Casino Advantage - 5.5% (2.8% when casinos pay 3 to 1 on either the 2 or 12)*

Big Six or Eight: Player wins if 6 or 8 is rolled before a 7; loses if a 7 is rolled before 6 or 8. The majority of casinos pay 1 to 1 on a win. *Casino Advantage - 9.1%.* A few casinos pay 7 to 6 on wagers of $6 or multiples thereof. In this case the casino advantage is the same as place bet to win (1.5%).

Any 7: One roll wager that can be made at any time. Wins if 7 is rolled on next dice roll; loses on any other number. Pays 4 to 1 on win. *Casino Advantage - 16.7%*

Any Craps: One roll wager that can be made at any time. The bet wins if a total of 2, 3, or 12 is rolled on next dice roll; loses on any other number. Pays 7 to 1 on win. *Casino Advantage - 11.1%*

Hardways: Bet can be made at any time on either hardway 4 (2, 2), 6 (3, 3), 8 (4, 4), or 10 (5, 5). Wins if the hardway number is rolled as a pair; loses if the same number is rolled in a non-pair combination or if a 7 is rolled before the hardway number comes up. *Casino Advantage - 9 to 11%*

Place Bet to Win: Wager can be made at any time on numbers 4, 5, 6, 8, 9 or 10. Wager wins if the place number is rolled before a 7; loses if a 7 is rolled before the place number. Pays 9 to 5 on 4 and 10; 7 to 5 on 5 and 9; and 7 to 6 on 6 and 8.
Casino Advantage -   1.5% on 6 & 8
4.0% on 5 & 9
6.7% on 4 & 10

Place Bet to Lose: Opposite of Place Bet to Win. Wager wins if 7 is rolled before the place number; loses if place number is rolled again before a 7. Pays 5 to 11 on 4 and 10; 4 to 5 on 5 and 9 and 5 to 8 on 6 or 8.
Casino Advantage -   1.8% on 6 & 8
2.5% on 5 & 9
3.0% on 4 & 10

Buy Bet: Same as Place Bet to Win, except payoff is 2 to 1 on 4 and 10; 3 to 2 on 5 and 9 and 6 to 5 on 6 and 8. A player pays a vigorish or commission of 5% of the bet to 'buy' the number. *Casino Advantage - 4.7%*

Lay Bet: Same as Place Bet to Lose. Commission is 5% of **the amount won**. Pays 1 to 2 on 4 and 10; 2 to 3 on 5 and 9; 5 to 6 on 6 and 8.

Casino Advantage - *2.4% on 4 & 10*
       3.2% on 5 and 9
       4.0% on 6 & 8

Craps Two: One roll wager that can be made at any time. Wins if 2 is rolled on next dice roll; loses on any other total. Pays 30 to 1. *Casino Advantage - 13.9%*

Craps Three; Craps 12; 11 in One Roll: Same won/lost principles as Craps Two. Pays 15 to 1 on 3; 30 to 1 on 12; 15 to 1 on 11. *Casino Advantage -* *11.1% on 3*
              13.9% on 12
              11.1% on 11

Odds Bet: Secondary bet that can be made on all pass line, don't pass, come and don't come bets. Pays 2 to 1 on 4 and 10; 3 to 2 on 5 and 9 and 6 to 5 on 6 and 8. *Casino Advantage - NONE*

There are two additional one roll combination bets that are popular:

C-E Bet: Player wagers that either craps (2, 3, 12) or 11 will be rolled on the next dice toss. Small C and E circles on the craps layout are used by the stickperson to position the bet.

Horn Bet: One roll wager that can be made at any time and wins if any of the totals 2, 3, 11 or 12 is thrown on next dice roll and loses on any other total. Bet must be made in multiples of 4 units. Pays off at 30 to 1 on 2 or 12; 15 to 1 on 3 or 11.

Appendix 2 contains a summary of craps bets and their casino advantage.

Recommended Bets

If you want to be a winner at craps you must limit your play to pass line, come, don't pass, don't come with odds. The only other bet you should ever consider is the place bets on the 6 and 8. All other crap bets should be avoided as the casino's edge is too high.

Odds Bet

Because of intense competition amongst casinos for craps players, many casinos are now offering what is known as multiple odds. Double odds, for example, is fairly common in which a casino allows a player to wager double the amount of their original pass line wager as odds. Many casinos are allowing triple odds, quintuple odds, and odds up to ten to twenty times the amount of the pass line wager.

Multiple odds reduce the casino's advantage significantly as the following chart shows:

	Casino advantage
Pass line	1.41%
Single odds	0.85%
Double odds	0.61%
Triple odds	0.47%
5 x odds	0.32%
10 x odds	0.18%
20 x odds	0.11%

Recommended Playing Strategy (beginners)

You should bet as little as possible on the pass line with maximum odds. The best strategy is $1 pass line bet with $10 or $20 in odds. Unfortunately the majority of the casinos only allow single, double or at best triple odds. In this case use the following playing and betting strategy:

Single Odds: Make a three chip wager on the pass line taking 3 chips as odds when the point is 4 or 10, 4 chips on 5 and 9, and 5 chips on 6 and 8. For example if your basic betting unit is $1, wager $3 on pass line taking $3 odds for 4 and 10, $4 odds for 5 and 9 and $5 odds for 6 and 8. A win pays $3 for pass line bet and $6 on odds bet.

Double Odds: Here your basic bet on pass line should be 2 units taking 4 units odds for the points 4, 5, 9, 10 and 5 units for 6 and 8. For example at a three dollar minimum bet table you should wager $4 on pass line and take $8 odds on 4, 5, 9, 10 and $10 odds for 6 and 8.

Triple Odds: For three dollar minimum bet tables, the casino will allow $10 in odds on all point numbers. On a $5 minimum bet table, the correct odds are $15 for 4, 6, 8, 10 and $18 for 5 and 9.

Don't let the above scare you. If you don't know how much to put as odds bet to get full odds payoff, simply ask the dealer for help. As a general rule the odds bet on the 5 and 9 should be made in even multiples (because of the 3 to 2 payoff) and for the 6 and 8, the odds should be in multiples of five (6 to 5 payoff).

After making the above pass line wagers you can make a come wager with odds. However, limit your play to pass line with two come bets all with maximum odds. If you are experiencing a good session and winning then and only then consider making a place bet on 6 or 8 if these numbers are not covered by come bets.

Use a 50% win progression for betting purposes. Whenever you win a bet, increase your next wager by 50% (i.e. if you win a $10 bet make your next bet $15). Whenever a loss is experienced, your next bet should be your minimum bet.

If you have a limited bankroll, you may want to try this strategy.

Make your first bet on pass line with single odds. If the bet wins, increase your odds to double. If it wins again, go to triple. Always keep the size of the pass line bet the same and increase your odds bet on successive wins. You can apply the same strategy for the come bet. This increased odds betting strategy is covered in more detail in my book, *Craps: Take the Money and Run*.

After you become experienced with the pass line and come bets, you may want to try the opposite don't pass and don't come bets using the above rules. Don't bettors are usually in the minority since it requires more capital outlay for odds bets (here you lay odds which means you bet more to win less since the don't bettor has the advantage once a point is established).

Other Points to Remember

- You can exchange cash for chips at the table. Every crap table has a chip rail to store your chips.

- You can only make a bet on the pass line on a come-out roll. Once a point is established you can wager on the come.

- You can remove your odds bet at any time but the pass and come bets must remain on the layout until a decision is rendered.

- Your pass line odds bet is made by placing your chips directly behind the original pass line bet. If unsure, ask the dealer for help.

- To make the odds bet on a come number, you place your odds bet in the come betting area and announce to the dealer to "put odds on the 6" (or whatever the come number was).

- Certain bets are not working on the come out roll. For example the odds bet on come and place bets are not working or are off on come out roll. You can, if you wish, tell the dealer you want those bets working on the come out roll.

- If you make a place bet on 6 or 8, you need to wager $6 and multiples of $6 ($12,18,24,etc.) The reason is that the 6 and 8 payoff at 7 to 6 (you win $7 for $6 bet). If one of your place bets wins, I suggest making the same bet again. If it wins again, I would increase from $6 to $12. After a third win, I would remove the bet from the layout (just tell the dealer to take your bet down).

- Craps is a fairly fast paced game with players making all kinds of bets on the layout. Ignore their betting patterns for many bet long shots with big payoffs but end up in the long run as big losers because they buck too high a casino advantage.

- Be patient at the crap table. Wait for a new shooter to make a point number *before* betting on the shooter. This avoids getting quickly wiped out on a "cold" table where the dice are passing (i.e. no one makes their point number).

- After a shooter "sevens out" (throws a seven before point number), the dice will pass clockwise to the next player. You do not have to throw the dice if you don't want to. If you do, pick up any two dice and throw them with enough force at the other end of the table so they rebound off the back wall.

- If you wager in the recommended manner, you'll be known as a tough player that with a little luck will wind up with many winning sessions.

- Another way to win money at craps is to enter a crap tournament. Here again it's important to learn specific tournament playing techniques (see Recommended Reading) to give yourself the best opportunity to end up in the final championship round.

Never Ever Craps

In this modified version of the standard game, you can't lose on 2, 3, or 12 on the come out roll. If a shooter throws one of these numbers it becomes the shooter's point, just like the 4, 5, 6, 8, 9, and 10 in the standard game. Also the natural 11 does not win on the come out roll like the standard game. It also becomes the shooter's point. This modified game is also known as crapless craps. The casino advantage on the pass line is higher (5.4%) then the standard game (1.4%).

Live Video Craps

Several casinos offer an electronic version of craps called Live Video Craps. The game is played on a rectangular table which contains a video screen that simulates the crap layout. However, the layout is different since you can't make don't pass and don't come bets. All other bets are allowed including single odds. Pass line bettors win if 7 is rolled on the come out throw. Any other number becomes the point, including the 2, 3, 12 and 11. Players use a trackball to place an arrow on the layout where they want to wager and then push a button to indicate the bet size. A pair of "electronic" dice will fly across the layout, bounce off the walls with sound effects, and come to rest. A computer generated voice announces the number rolled and a rake appears on the layout which simulates sweeping away the losing bets.

The game is fairly easy to learn how to play and the minimum bet (usually 25 cents or $1) is lower than the regular table. The overall casino advantage on the pass line is about 5% which is more than the 1.4% available in the standard game.

Crap Shoot

This mini craps table was developed by several employees at Harrah's casino in Atlantic City. Up to 9 players seat comfortably around a semi-oval 9 foot crap table where they can play craps just like in the big game. Only one dealer is required to run the game and the unique layout contains all of the bets available in the regular game. Besides the obvious comfort of sitting while playing rather than standing, the game is much less intimidating to new players. It is an excellent way for a beginner to get started playing craps and I highly recommend the game.

Final Thoughts

Don't be impressed with other crap players when they start throwing their chips on the table instructing the dealers to bet them on C-E (craps/eleven), hardways, yo'leven, etc. Likewise high rollers will always bet all the numbers once a point is established hoping for a quick kill. The plain fact of the matter is sometimes, but not often, these players will win big but the high casino advantage will eventually result in their losing money over the long run. Your best strategy for playing and winning at craps is as follows: be patient by waiting for a shooter to make a point before betting, make bets with the lowest possible casino edge, increase your bets only when winning (never when losing), setting a limit on losses should the worst happen, and if the dice are rolling your way, disciplining yourself to take the profits and run!

"Anyone coming to the crap table with a couple of hundred dollars can, with luck and a hot roll, walk away with ten or twenty thousand dollars."

Edwin Silberstang

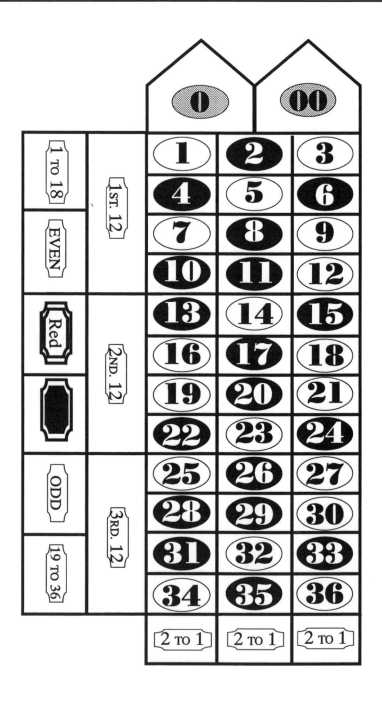

5

ROULETTE

The casino game of roulette has its origins in the great gambling palaces of Europe where the game was traditionally played by both prince and pauper since the 17th century. It is the most elegant and more popular of the European casino games but here in the United States the game has never enjoyed this vast popularity because the house percentage is greater than in Europe. But still the game has its advantages—the rules are easy to learn, it's an easy game to play and it offers the player an opportunity to play in a relaxed atmosphere unlike the noisy atmosphere at craps or the tense atmosphere at blackjack.

Objective

To guess in which number pocket the roulette ball will land.

Roulette Chips
Special colored roulette chips are used at each table. A player can purchase these roulette chips at the table with cash or regular casino chips. Every seated player receives a different colored stack of these chips. You must cash these chips in at the table before leaving.

Types of Bets
The following describes the bets available, the rules for winning and losing, and the payoffs:

Inside Bets:
One-Number Bet: Wager on a particular number. Pays 35 to 1.

Two-Number Bet: Wager on two adjacent numbers. Pays 17 to 1.

Three-Number Bet: Wager on three adjacent numbers. Pays 11 to 1.

Four-Number Bet: Wager on four adjacent numbers. Pays 8 to 1.

Five-Number Bet: Wager on 0, 00, 1, 2 and 3. Pays 6 to 1.

Six-Number Bet: Wager on six adjacent numbers. Pays 5 to 1.

Outside Bets:
Column Bet: Wager on any 12 numbers in a single column. Pays 2 to 1.

Dozens Bet: Wager on first dozen (1 thru 12); second dozen

(13 thru 24); or third dozen (25 thru 36). Pays 2 to 1.

Red or Black: Wager on either red number or black number. Wins when bet color matches winning number color. Pays 1 to 1.

Odd or Even: Wager on either even number or odd number. Pays 1 to 1.

Low or High: Wager that winning number will be either low (1 to 18) or high (19-36). Pays 1 to 1.

Positioning Your Chips

It's important that you know where to position your chips on the layout depending upon the type of bet you want to make.

For example, if you want to make a two number wager on the numbers 20 and 21, you do so by placing your chip(s) on the line that separates these two numbers. Likewise if you wish to wager on four numbers 32, 33, 35 and 36, you place your chips at the intersection of those numbers.

Casinos provide free brochures that show the placement of all roulette bets or just ask the dealer.

Since all players have their own color roulette chips, it's easy to know which bet belongs to whom. You can also place your chips on top of someone else's if they happen to be making the same bet.

Minimum/Maximum Bets

Casinos normally have a placard that stipulates what are the table minimum and maximum bets.

Usually if the table has a $5 minimum bet requirement, this is the minimum bet a player can make on bets on the outside of the layout (e.g. red/black). On the inside bets (bets on a number or combination of numbers), a player can wager less than $5 on any one bet but the total of the inside bets must be at least $5. For example you could wager $1 straight up on number 7, $1 straight up on number 11, $1 on 25/26, and $2 on 20,21,23,24. This player has a total of four inside bets totaling $5.

When to Bet

Even after the roulette dealer has launched the roulette ball, players can continue to bet. As the ball loses momentum, the dealer will announce "no more bets." After the ball lands in one of the pockets, the dealer announces the winning number and puts a market on the layout on top of the winning number. The dealer will then go through a process of sweeping the losing chips from the layout then carefully paying off the winning bets in an exact sequence (outside bets get paid first, then inside bets). The dealer will give the winning chips on inside bets directly to the player. On outside bets, the dealer will stack the chips next to the original bet on the layout. Do not pick up your winning chips from the layout or start to make new bets until the dealer has completed paying off all bets and removes the marker from the layout.

Single and Double O Wheels

The vast majority of roulette wheels have a zero and double zero pocket. This is known as a double O wheel. The casino's advantage for all the bets described above is 5.26% except the five number bet which has a 7.89% casino advantage and should be avoided. Casinos which offer a single O wheel are a better bet. Here the casino's advantage is cut in half to 2.63%. Some casinos, such as those in Atlantic City, have a special rule that allows only one half of the wager to be lost on outside bets on the double zero wheel whenever the ball lands on zero or double zero (so called surrender rule). These outside bets include those wagers that payoff at 1 to 1: red/black, odd/even, or high/low. This special rule for double zero wheels reduces the casino advantage for these even payoff bets to 2.70%. European casinos allow surrender or the similar en prison rule on their single zero wheels which reduces the casino advantage to about 1.4%. This is why roulette is more popular in Europe than in the states. Very few casinos in the USA offer the European single zero wheel with the en prison option. However, from time to time some casinos offer this more player favorable roulette game. Given a choice, play on a single zero wheel if available.

Recommendation

Your best bet is to play on a single O wheel. If that's not available, play the outside bets on a double zero wheel that allows the surrender rule. Your last choice is the double zero wheel.

Playing Systems

There are literally hundreds of betting systems that have been designed to try to overcome the casino advantage. Of course these systems can't do this and in the long run a roulette player is doomed to lose. However, systems play does have one advantage. It disciplines a player to make a series of predetermined bets rather than betting haphazardly over the layout. And if your lucky numbers hit, be smart and leave the table with your winnings.

Recommended Playing System

Outside Bets (high/low, red/black, even/odd):
1. Make your first bet the table minimum on any of the outside wagers (assume 1 chip bet).
2. If you win, let your winnings ride on the next spin (you now bet 2 chips).
3. If you win again, the dealer will pay 2 chips. Take one of these chips, add it to the original 2 chip bet and now wager 3 chips on the same bet. The single winning chip

left is set aside. At this point you are basically wagering with profits.

4. If you win again, the dealer pays you 3 chips. Make your next bet four chips, and set aside 2 chips as profit.

5. Keep betting in this manner, adding one chip to your bet if it wins and setting aside the rest as profit.

6. If you lose at any point, go back to the original starting bet of one chip and start over.

7. Stack your chips in increments of five (or ten). Concentrate first on doubling your initial buy-in, then stack your chips in increments of fives and play with only the odd number of chips left. If you win five more chips, add them to your profits. If you lose the odd chips you have left, leave the table with your profits (which should amount to your initial buy-in plus an equal amount of chips as profit).

This simple betting system on the outside bets on roulette will yield substantial profits if you are lucky enough to get a streak of 4 or more wins in a row.

Another playing system I can suggest is to bet on the dozens as follows:

Betting the Dozens

1. Make your first bet one chip on any one of the three dozen of numbers (first dozen covers numbers 1 through 12, the second dozen covers 13 through 24, and the third dozen covers 25 through 36).

2. If you win the bet, you will be paid 2 chips as winnings. Take one of your winning chips and play it on a second dozen of numbers. Take the second winning chip and set it aside. Leave the one initial one chip on the original dozen of numbers on the layout (you now have 2 dozens covered by one chip each).

3. If one of the two dozens of numbers that you have covered wins, the dealer will pay you 2 chips for the winning dozens

bet and collect the one chip from the other losing dozens bet. Take one of your winning chips and put it back on the dozen of numbers that just lost and set the second chip aside.

4. If you win again, the dealer will remove one chip and pay you two. Again replace the losing dozen of numbers with a chip and pull back the second chip.

5. From the last two winning coups you have two chips set aside. Take these two chips and add one to each of the dozen of numbers so that now you will have 2 chips riding on each dozen of numbers.

6. If you win again, repeat the process. Keep two chips aside and replace the losing dozen bet with two chips. Win again and increase your bets on the two dozen of numbers to three chips. After three more winning spins, increase your bets to four chips on each dozen of numbers. The progression continues in the same manner: 4 consecutive wins, then increase to 5 chips; 5 consecutive wins, then increase to 6 chips, etc.

This method of betting will allow you to keep part of the profits and use the rest to gradually increase your bet size. After 4 consecutive wins you will have a 2 chip profit. After 5 consecutive wins your profit is 3 chips and so on. At any time you lose both of the dozen bets, revert back to the basic one chip bet and start the progression over.

If you analyze this betting method you will see it involves increasing bets following consecutive wins with some of your profits, a predetermined method of betting and decreasing the bet size following a loss so as not to chase losses. With a little luck and patience it is a smart way to bet in roulette.

Inside Bets

For betting the numbers, I recommend the Shotwell roulette system. Here's how it's played:

The Shotwell system is a method of controlling your betting on the *inside numbers* at the roulette table. The chart below describes a series of betting strategies with an interesting result. With one four number bet and four one-number bets the player can cover the wheel within three spaces of every possible number. Your odds against winning are 4 to 1 but your casino advantage stays the same at 5.26%.

SIX NUMBER COMBINATIONS AND THE FOUR NUMBERS STRAIGHT UP

1 through 6	also play numbers	20, 26, 8, and 10
4 through 9	"	13, 14, 15, and 10
10 through 15	"	16, 17, 18, and 28
13 through 18	"	11, 12, 27, and 28
19 through 24	"	1, 2, 4, and 26
28 through 33	"	00, 22, 24, and 35
31 through 36	"	0, 00, 29, and 30

Biased vs. Unbiased Roulette Wheels

An unbiased roulette wheel means that there is no mechanical defects which could alter the probabilities of the roulette ball landing in any of the numbered pockets. Roulette wheels are meticulously manufactured and regularly checked by mechanics in the casinos to maintain their integrity. As long as the wheel remains unbiased, the casinos will continue to maintain their rather large edge over the players and can't lose. However, there have been reported cases of players charting roulette wheels to find a biased wheel. This charting of the winning roulette numbers generally is done by a team of individuals on a continuous basis for days on end. Once their data indicate a particular number on a particular wheel is occurring more frequently than the probability dictates they then begin to wager first small then large sums of money on these biased wheels. The cause of these bias wheels could be due to any number of defects such as a loose fret (or metal wall) that separates the pockets or badly worn pockets. These defects can cause the ball to land more frequently on certain numbers than others. Only charting will be able to spot these biases. In 1986, the Billy Walters Syndicate charted roulette tables at the Golden Nugget Casino in Atlantic City for several days, found a biased wheel and started betting $2000 on each of five numbers (total of $10,000 per spin). After a total of 18 hours of play covering a day and a half, Mr. Walters and his team were ahead three million eight hundred thousand dollars! This was the largest sum ever won at a biased roulette wheel.

It is therefore possible to have a substantial edge over the casino in roulette but it requires a lot of time and effort to chart roulette wheels. For those wishing to pursue this adventure, I highly recommend the book *Beating the Wheel* by Russell Barnhart.

If you'd like to try charting roulette numbers I can recommend the following playing strategy. It involves charting the winning roulette numbers for 38 consecutive spins. Although this is not nearly enough data for a detailed study of biases, you may get lucky and discover a bias using it.

Place the following numbers on a piece of paper or on the roulette scorecard in exact order as written.

9, 26, 30, 11, 7, 20, 32, 17, 5, 22, 34, 15, 3, 24, 36,
13, 1, 00, 27, 10, 25, 29, 12, 8, 19, 31, 18, 6, 21, 33,
16, 4, 23, 35, 14, 2, 0, 28

These numbers represent the exact sequence of the roulette numbers as they appear around the wheel. Simply observe the winning number for 38 spins and put a tick mark next to that number on your scorecard. Most casinos have electronic monitors that show the last 15 or so winning numbers to make your job easier (just tick off these numbers on your scorecard and then observe the next 21 or so spins).

After charting 38 spins, pick out the dominant number or that number that has won more than any other. Wager as follows:

1. Bet one chip on the dominant number and one chip each on two adjacent numbers that appear on the roulette wheel to left of dominant number and one chip each on two adjacent numbers to right of dominant number (for example, if 11 is dominant number, bet also on 26, 30, 7, 20). You should have five bets on the layout on five numbers straight up.

2. If one of your bets wins, (pays 35 to 1) use part of your profits to increase your bets to two chips on the same five numbers.

3. As long as one (or more) bets continues to win, increase your bets on the five numbers as follows: 1 chip, 2, 4, 8, 16, etc.

4. When none of the numbers wins, drop back to 1 chip wager on each of the 5 numbers.

5. Buy in for 40 chips. That gives you 8 spins to hopefully hit a winning number. If none of your numbers hit, limit your loss to 40 chips.

6. If a few numbers hit, you'll start to pile up profits. After a few no hits, plan to "take the profits and run."

Final Tips

• Normally you establish the value of your roulette chips by how much money you give the dealer for a standard stack of 20 roulette chips. If you give the dealer $20, then each of your roulette chips in the stack of 20 will be worth $1. If you gave the dealer $10, then each of your chips will be worth 50 cents. The dealer keeps track of the worth of each of your chips with a marker that is set on top (or next to) the roulette wheel.

- Roulette chips have no value elsewhere in the casino. You must cash in your roulette chips at the roulette table and in return you'll receive the equivalent value of regular casino chips. The latter can be used elsewhere in the casino or cashed out at the casino cashier for currency.

- If you can't reach an area of the layout where you want to place your chips, simply instruct the dealer and he/she will make the bet.

- Sometimes the casino will allow players to wager with regular casino chips. But this is not preferred because it becomes difficult for the dealer to keep track of which bet belongs to whom. It's best if you are going to play roulette for any length of time, to purchase and use roulette chips.

Summary

To reduce the casino's advantage to as low as possible, play roulette on a European single zero wheel vs. the American standard double zero wheel. In Atlantic City casinos, bet on the 1 to 1 payoff wagers to take advantage of the surrender rule. The only other way to lower the casino's edge is to play on a bias wheel.

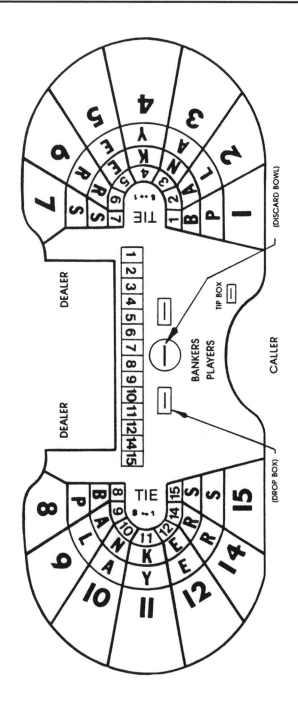

6

BACCARAT

Baccarat is a unique casino game because of its rather low and fixed casino advantage. The latter means no matter what the player does or how they bet, the casino's edge will be no greater than 1.3% (except for betting on the tie which should be avoided because of its high 14% edge). A game this close can be beaten over the short run by skillful players. In fact from the casino's perspective, baccarat is a real gamble because large losses to high rolling baccarat players can negatively effect their bottom line.

Objective

Two hands are dealt in baccarat - the bank hand and the player hand. Prior to the deal, each player wagers on either the bank hand or the player hand (or on the tie bet). Whichever of the two hands (bank or player) is closest to 9 is the winner.

Bets Available

There are only three. A player may wager on bank hand, player hand, or tie bet.

Card Values

All tens and picture cards equal zero. The ace equals 1. Remaining cards count face value. Two or a maximum of three cards are dealt to the player hand and bank hand. If the value of cards exceed 9, then the value is adjusted by subtracting 10 from the total (for example, 9,6 hand has a value of 5).

Payoffs

Winning player hand wagers are paid 1 to 1. Winning bank hand wagers are paid 1 to 1 but the player must pay a 5% commission. Winning tie hand wagers are paid at 8 to 1.

Third Card Draw

Either or both player and bank hand may require a third card draw, however, the decision for drawing a third card is not made by the players. They are dictated by set rules. The third card rules are as follows:

PLAYER HAND THIRD CARD RULES

If Player Hand Two Card Total is:	Then Player Hand:
0, 1, 2, 3, 4, 5	DRAWS A CARD
6, 7	STANDS
8, 9	NATURAL STANDS

After the player hand acts on a third card draw, the bank hand receives a third card according to these rules:

If Bank Hand Card Total is:	Bank Hand Draws When Players Third Card is:	Bank Hand Stands When Players Third Card is:
0, 1, 2	BANK HAND ALWAYS DRAWS	
3	0, 1, 2, 3, 4, 5, 6, 7, 9	8
4	2, 3, 4, 5, 6, 7	0, 1, 8, 9
5	4, 5, 6, 7	0, 1, 2, 3, 8, 9
6	6, 7	0, 1, 2, 3, 4, 5, 8, 9
7	BANKER ALWAYS STANDS	
8, 9	NATURAL-BANK STANDS	

If the player hand stands on two cards then two card bank hand totaling 3, 4, 5 must *draw* and 6 must *stand*.

Casino Advantage

Based on a mathematical analysis of the game, bank hand will win 45.8% of the time, player hand 44.6%, and tie 9.6%. If we discount the ties, bank hand stands to win 50.7% of the time and player hand 49.3%. Since the bank hand wins greater than 50% of the time, the casinos compensate for this advantage by charging a 5% commission every time you win a bank hand bet. The net result is that casino's advantage is 1.17% for bank hand and 1.36% for the player hand. The bank hand is therefore a slightly better bet. The casino's edge on the tie bet is a whopping 14.1% and should be avoided.

3 and 4% Commissions

Several casinos in Las Vegas reduce their commissions on winning bank hand bets from 5% to 4 and even 3%. The Horseshoe Casino in downtown Las Vegas usually offers a 4% commission game on a regular basis. This reduced commission significantly reduces the casino's advantage.

	Casino Advantage on Bank Hand
5% Commission	1.17%
4% Commission	0.67%
3% Commission	0.16%

Baccarat Card Counting

Through the monumental computer studies of Dick Rahm and I, a system for card counting at baccarat was developed. It is beyond the scope of this book to describe the system in detail. Suffice it to say that our studies indicate that the cards more favorable to the bank hand are the 9, 8, 10, J, Q, K in order of strength and the 4, 3, 2, 5 are player favorable cards. Our counting system follows the imbalance of these cards in the shoe as the game progresses. The count is used for hand selection. When the count is positive, then the better bet is the bank hand; when the count is negative, the player hand is the better bet.

There is a big difference between card counting in blackjack vs. baccarat. In blackjack, a counting system is used to determine if the shoe favors the casino or the player. In baccarat, the shoe almost always favors the casino. Thus we use a counting system in baccarat to determine which hand (bank or player) the casino earns the smaller percentage, and then wager on it. In short, baccarat card counting is used to reduce the casino's advantage over the player. As such, it is an effective playing strategy much like the basic playing strategy is for the game of blackjack.

For those that wish to learn more about baccarat card counting, I suggest you consult our book, *Winning Baccarat Strategies* which explains this strategy in detail.

Mini-baccarat

Many casinos offer a lower stakes game of baccarat on a table similar to a blackjack table. In mini-baccarat the dealer deals all the cards unlike the regular baccarat where the players deal the cards. Also mini-baccarat tables are usually located in the main casino area next to the other table games and the play is less formal than the regular game. The playing rules are identical to the regular game.

Other Tidbits

• The maximum number of cards that either the bank hand or player hand may have is 3.

• If you wager on either bank or player hand and the hands tie (same total) then your bet is a push or tie (you don't lose the bet). Of course if you wagered on a tie bet, you'd win.

• Always remember to have enough money to pay off the commissions on the winning bank hand. It would be very embarrassing to lose all your money, then as you are ready to leave the table be reminded by the dealer that you still owe the markers in the commission box.

• Baccarat is a fast game. It's not uncommon to have 5 hands/min. It's also a game of streaks where consecutive wins on either bank or player hand are common.

• Baccarat is the game for high rollers who like to make very large bets and have quick decisions on the outcome. The most prominent of the baccarat high rollers, Mr. Akio Kashiwagi (who was recently killed) and Mr. Ken Mizuno, were capable of betting $200,000 per hand over a period of several days. It's been reported that Mizuno lost around $65 million over a two year period in Las Vegas and Kashiwagi died owing $9 million in gambling losses to several casinos in Las Vegas and Atlantic City.

Recommended Playing Strategy

The optimum strategy is to play in a 3 or 4% commission game. Baccarat tends to be streaky and to capitalize on successive bank or player hand wins, I would suggest the following strategy.

Using the scorecard that casinos provide all players, keep track of which hand won. When you are ready to make your bet, simply bet on the hand that won last. In other words, if the bank hand just won, make your next bet on the bank hand. The decision as to which hand to bet on is thus predetermined depending upon the sequence of wins or loses as the hands are played. By betting in this manner you'll always be betting on the hand that's streaking. Along with this hand selection system, increase your bets gradually on consecutive wins but whenever a loss occurs revert back to your minimum bet.

No Commission Game

Several casinos are trying to eliminate the commission on bank hand wins, which players dislike, by slightly changing the rules. In one version, when the bank hand totals 4 and players hand totals 0, 1, 2, or 3, the hand is a tie. It remains to be seen if these modified versions of the standard game will gain wide acceptance amongst baccarat players.

"Baccarat offers you your best shot to win money in the casino. Although it is often played for incredibly high stakes, it can also be played for as little as a few dollars a hand. The size of your wager isn't important. Your knowledge of the game is."

Lyle Stuart

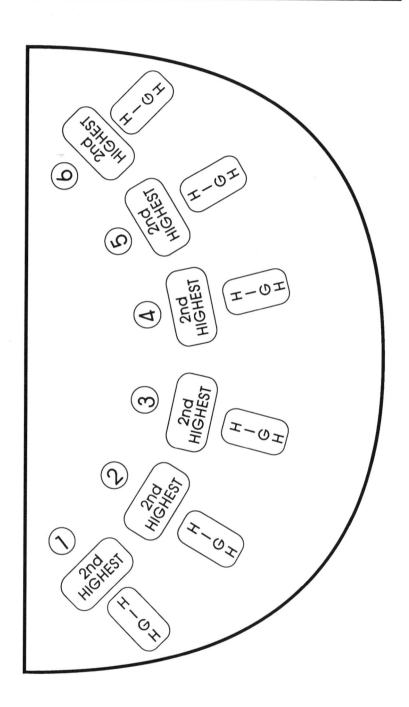

7

PAI GOW POKER

Objective

For both of the player's two hands to rank higher than both of the banker's two hands.

Hands

Players receive seven cards and must make two traditional poker hands. The high hand is made up of five cards and the low hand contains two cards.

Hand Rankings

The rankings of the two hands are based upon a basic poker ranking. Thus the highest two card hand is two aces and the highest five card hand is a royal flush.

Mechanics of Play

One standard deck of 52 cards plus one joker is used. The joker is not wild but can be used only as an ace or as a card to complete a straight, flush, a straight flush or royal flush.

The dealer shuffles and deals seven hands of seven cards each face down. A dice cup containing three dice is shaken and used to determine who receives the first hand. The dealer's position is always 1, 8 or 15 and rotation is counterclockwise.

After all the players receive their seven cards, they must form the two hands. The low hand must contain two cards and the high hand five cards. The most important rule to remember when playing is that the rank of the five card high hand must be higher than the two card low hand. Any player's hand that is set incorrectly will automatically lose.

The casino dealer sets the bank hand according to fixed house rules. Once all hands are set, the dealer will compare the players hand rank with his or her hands. To win your wager, your low hand and high hand must both rank higher than the dealer's low and high hands. If one of your hands is higher in rank than the dealer's and the other is lower, this is a tie and your bet remains on the layout. If the dealer beats both of your hands, then you lose your wager. If both hands are identical (copy hands), the dealer also wins.

Commission

Every time a player wins they are paid even money less a 5% commission. No commission is collected on losing hands or ties.

The Banker

Any player may be the banker and wager against all other players and the dealer. Casinos have different rules on how many times a player can act as banker. Normally, the dealer will ask each player in turn if they wish to be the banker and the same player can't bank two consecutive hands. If a player requests to be banker, the player must have sufficient chips to cover all the other player wagers.

Co-banking

At the banker's request, the casino will co-bank at 50/50. When co-banking, the banker's hand will be set according to the same casino rules that the dealers must use to set their hand.

Poker Rankings

The following rankings are used to determine the higher hand:

Five Aces (four aces plus joker)
Royal Flush
Straight Flush
Four of a Kind
Full House
Flush
Straight
Three of a Kind
Two Pair
One Pair
High Card

Recommended Playing Strategy

The dealer (or banker) must set his cards by specific casino rules. However, the players can set their hands any way they wish. Computer studies have been done to determine the optimum way to set both hands. Here are some tips on how to best set your hand depending on what type of hand you are dealt (i.e. a hand that contains no pairs, one pair, two pairs, etc.).

No Pairs: Play the second- and third-highest-ranked cards as the low hand and the remaining five cards as high hand. For example if you were dealt ace, 10, 5, 9, 3, 2, J, you would set the J, 10 as low hand and ace, 5, 9, 3, 2 as high hand.

One Pair: The pair is set in the high hand and your next two highest-ranked cards as low hand. For example 3, 3, 5, 7, 9, K, 10 you would play 3, 3, 5, 7, 9 as high hand and K, 10 as low hand.

Two Pair: Your playing strategy depends upon the rank of the pairs. If one of your pairs is A, A; K, K; Q, Q, then split the pairs putting the high pair (As, Ks, Qs) in high hand and the other pair as low hand. For all other pairs, play them as two pair in the high hand if you have a king or ace that you can use in your low hand. If you don't have a king or ace, then you're better off to split the pairs with the high pair in high hand and low pair in low hand.

Three Pair: Play your highest-ranking pair in low hand.

Three-of-a-kind: With three aces and kings, split them playing the ace (or king) in low hand and the pair in high hand. All other ranked three-of-a-kind should be played in high hand with your two highest-ranked cards as the low hand.

Straights and Flushes: In general, play the straight or flush as the high hand, the remaining two cards as low hand.

Full House: Play the high pair as low hand and the three-of-a-kind in high hand.

Four-of-a-kind: Always split your four As, Ks, Qs–play one pair as low hand and the other in high hand. With four Js-7s, play them as a four-of-a-kind in high hand only if you have at least a queen that you can use in low hand. If you don't have the latter, then split the four-of-a-kind (two in low hand, two in high hand). With four 2s-6s, never split, always play them in high hand.

Five Aces: Strange as this may seem, you should split the aces and play a pair of aces in low hand, and three aces in high hand.

Casino Advantage

The casino's advantage against an average player is about 2.8%. If the player uses the above strategies to set hands the casino's edge can be lowered to about 2.5%. The key to reducing the casino's edge is to try to be the banker as much as feasible and use the optimum strategy for setting hands. It is theoretically possible for a skillful banker to play with an even game against the casino (casino has no advantage) and in some cases to actually have a slight 0.3% edge against the casino. To accomplish this you must try to be the banker as often as the casino allows and always bet the minimum when you have to be the player. Complete details on how to get the edge in pai gow poker are contained in Stanford Wong's excellent book, *Optimal Strategy for Pai Gow Poker*.

Recommendation

Learn the optimum playing strategies for setting your hands, bet the minimum when you are the player and try to bank often.

	1st Coin	2nd Coin	3rd Coin	4th Coin	5th Coin
Royal Flush	250	500	750	1000	4000
Straight Flush	50	100	150	200	250
4 of a Kind	25	50	75	100	125
Full House	9	18	27	36	45
Flush	6	12	18	24	30
Straight	4	8	12	16	20
3 of a Kind	3	6	9	12	15
2 Pair	2	4	6	8	10

Bet Returned on Jacks or Better

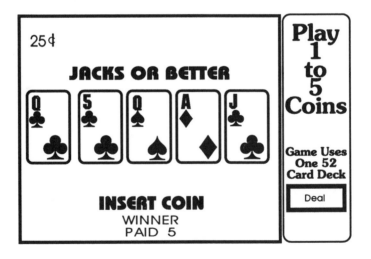

8

VIDEO POKER

Video Poker has established considerable growth over the past several years. Just walk into any casino and you'll see rows and rows of these video marvels. To be successful at playing these machines you will need to learn to play at machines with the highest payback and learn a playing strategy for which cards to hold and which to discard.

Objective

To make the highest five card ranking poker hand.

Which Machine to Play

All video poker machines are *not* created equal. Although the probabilities of getting a specific poker hand on these machines does not change, what does is the payback. For example the most popular video poker machines are the ones that pay back if a player gets at least a pair of jacks or higher hand. When you play these machines, check first the payback on the screen before you play. The highest payback machines are those that pay 9 coins for a full house and 6 coins for a flush for a single coin played. The five coin royal flush jackpot should be 4,000 coins. These machines are known as 9/6 machines and they offer you the highest theoretical payback for perfect play (99.6%). The 8/6, 7/5, 6/5 payoff machines yield a lower payback for expert play. Given a choice, play only those machines with the highest payback.

How to Play

This is the easy part. You can either insert coins into the machines or nowadays most machines will accept bills. The newer machines will total your winnings as credit which you can receive in coins at any time by pressing the cash out button. After you've inserted the coins, press the deal button. Five cards appear on the screen. You can select which cards to keep (or hold) by pressing the hold button beneath the respective cards. Pushing the draw button will replace the cards not held with new cards. In video poker you can discard as many cards as you like (all five if you want). Remember the name of the game is to end up with at least a pair of jacks (or higher) poker hand for a payoff.

Rank of Hands

The higher the rank of the hand the greater the payoff. Therefore it is important you understand the rankings. In descending order the rankings are: royal flush, straight flush, 4 of a kind, full house, flush, straight, 3 of a kind, 2 pair, jacks or better.

Payouts

The payouts for each of the above hands are listed on the screen. The maximum number of coins you can play is normally 5 coins. It is a good idea to play the maximum number to be eligible for the bonus payout on the royal flush.

Playing Strategy

The following is a simplified playing strategy for the popular jacks or better machines. It's not a complete playing strategy but it's enough to get you started.

Just start at the top of the chart and go down until you find your hand. Follow the strategy listed.

1. Keep any full house or better.
2. Draw one card to a four card royal flush (even if it means breaking up a flush or straight).
3. Hold any flush or straight.
4. Draw one to any four card straight flush.
5. Draw two to three of a kind (do not keep a kicker).
6. Draw one to two pair.
7. Draw three to any high pair (jacks through aces). If your hand has three different high cards, keep only two and draw three.
8. Draw one to a four card flush.
9. Draw two to any three card royal flush.
10. Draw three to any pair of tens or less.
11. Draw one to any four card straight.
12. Draw two to any three straight flush.
13. Draw three to any two high cards (jacks or better).
14. Draw four cards to a high card (jacks or better).
15. Draw five new cards.

Summary of Different Video Poker Games

Jacks or Better These machines have no wild card and their pay tables begin with a pair of jacks. As mentioned earlier, machines that pay 9 coins for full house and 6 coins for flush have an overall payback of 99.6%. Machines that pay less than 9/6 such as 8/5, 7/5, etc. yield a lower theoretical payback. As a general rule, the payback is cut 1.1% for each one unit below the 9/6 payback (an 8/5 machine has an overall theoretical payback of 97.4%).

Deuces Wild. With these machines, deuces are wild. One of the best payback machines are ones that offer a minijackpot of 200 to

1 for four deuces and the following pay schedule (per coin played).

Royal Flush	800 coins
Four Deuces	200
Deuce Royal	25
5 of a Kind	15
Straight Flush	9
4 of a Kind	5
Full House	3
Flush	2
Straight	2
3 of a Kind	1

The payback for this machine is 100.6% with expert play.

Progressive Machines. These jacks or better machines pay large progressive jackpots for a royal flush. The best pay 8 coins for a full house and 5 for a flush.

Bonus Video Poker. These relatively new machines are growing in popularity. They basically pay a bonus for four of a kind combinations at the expense of paying less for other winning hands. For example, in a regular jacks or better game, 4 of a kind pays $125 (five coin dollar machine), whereas in some bonus poker machines the payoffs increase to $400 for four aces, and $200 for four 2's, 3's, or 4's. The best Bonus Poker machines pay 8 coins for a full house and 5 for the flush, with the above bonus for quads (4 of a kind). The payback on these machines is 99.2%.

Double or Nothing. This option is showing up on more video poker machines. After you win a hand, the video screen will ask if you want to try to double your winnings. If you select yes, the screen will show one card (the dealer's card) faced and four other cards. Your objective is to select one of the four cards and hope the value of the card is greater than the dealer's card. If it is, your winnings are doubled. If it's lower, you've lost your winnings.

If you get lucky and win a few double or nothing bets, it will keep you on the machine longer. On the downside, if you lose those bets, your playing time will be very short.

Joker Poker. This game is played with a standard 52 card deck plus a wild card Joker. It is a highly volatile game which means you can experience long losing streaks followed by big wins. There are many different payoff Joker Poker machines. One of the very best is the 20-8-7-6 two pair or better machines that pay 4,000 coins for a natural royal flush with the maximum coins played.

The following is the pay table for these machines (per coin played).

Natural Royal Flush	800 coins
5 of a Kind	100
Joker Royal Flush	50
Straight Flush	50
4 of a Kind	20
Full House	8
Flush	7
Straight	6
3 of a Kind	2
Two Pairs	1

The payback for this machine is 101.6% with expert play.

Recommendation

Given a choice, play only those machines with the highest payback (return). Always play the maximum coins allowed to get the benefit of a bonus payout for the royal flush. Stick with one type of machine (e.g. jacks or better) and learn the optimum playing strategy for that game.

Joker
45 to 1

$10	$20	$10	$20	$10
10 to 1	20 to 1	10 to 1	20 to 1	10 to 1
$5	$5	$5	$5	$5
5 to 1	5 to 1	5 to 1	5 to 1	5 to 1
$2	$2	$2	$2	$2
2 to 1	2 to 1	2 to 1	2 to 1	2 to 1
$1	$1	$1	$1	$1
1 to 1	1 to 1	1 to 1	1 to 1	1 to 1

9

Big 6 Wheel

Objective

To guess at which number or symbol the wheel will stop.

Layout

There are 54 stops on the big six wheel. A player wagers on any number, the dealer spins the wheel and pays off the number at which the wheel stops. A player can make as many bets as he likes. The payoffs and casino advantage for the bets are:

Bet	Payoff	Casino Advantage
$ 1 Slot	1 to 1	14.8%
$ 2 Slot	2 to 1	16.7%
$ 5 Slot	5 to 1	11.1%
$10 Slot	10 to 1	18.5%
$20 Slot	20 to 1	22.2%
$Joker	45 to 1	14.8%
$Flag	45 to 1	14.8%

Advantage

The only advantage the big six wheel has over the other table games is its low stakes. Normally, the minimum bet is only $1 and this usually attracts low stakes bettors.

Recommendation

Even at $1 a spin, don't play this game unless you are willing to find a biased wheel by charting (see below). The high casino advantage for an unbiased wheel will cause you to lose over the long run.

Biased-Wheel

Sometimes, but not often, certain numbers win with more frequency on specific wheels. This may be caused by defects in the wheel (fret, flapper, etc) or by the repetitive spinning of the wheel by a tired dealer. The only way to find a biased wheel is to chart the winning numbers similar to the earlier discussions on roulette. If the dealer spins the wheel in the same pattern it's easy to spot by noting how many times the joker goes through one revolution and how far in the last revolution. For example, if a tired or bored dealer always spins the wheel 4 to 4½ revolutions, then wherever the wheel stops count that many revolutions and make bets within a range of 5 to 10 numbers from where you predict the winning number to be. Always chart the wheel and dealer *before* making any bets to be *certain* you have found a bias or pattern.

"My advice is to admire the big six wheel in action, especially if the casino owns one that is antique and ornate, but don't put good money on it."

Edwin Silberstang

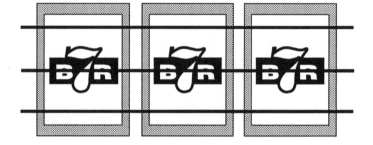

10

SLOT MACHINES

Objective

    To line up the symbols on the reels for the highest possible payoff.

How They Work

    Modern slot machines operate by computer. Every millisecond the computer is generating a series of random numbers (known as the random number generator, or RNG). These numbers randomly selected by the RNG are correlated to the different symbols on each reel. The casino can determine this correlation (by computer programming) and ultimately the probability of each symbol appearing on the payline. Usually, the probabilities for each symbol are *not* the same. Some symbols are programmed to "hit" more often than other symbols. Based on these programmed probabilites and the posted payoffs, the casino can set any desired advantage. The point that is important to remember is that each spin and outcome is an independent process. It doesn't matter what the previous results were, or how many coins are played, or who is playing the machines. You cannot predict the results of the next spin - it is a completely random process.

Linked Machines

The new video progressive slot machines are linked together such that every coin played results in an increase in the jackpot. It's common to find million dollar progressive jackpots in most casinos. If you play these machines always play the maximum coins to have a chance at the bonus jackpot payoff.

Which Machines to Play

As a slot player you have a choice of which casino and machine to play. Your best bet is to play in casinos that tend to cater to slot machine players. For example in Las Vegas, the average slot payoffs are slightly higher in the casinos in the downtown area than the strip.

When it comes to which machine, you have a choice of playing a machine that pays a lot of smaller payoffs vs. those that have a larger jackpot and less frequent smaller payoffs. You can always tell which machine is what by looking at the payout schedules. Unfortunately what you can't tell is which machines payout percentage is greater. On quarter machines for example, some machines payout 95.6% of all the coins that are played. Other machines payout percentage may be only 93.6% or less. Although it's virtually impossible to know the specific payout percentages on each machine (only the casino managers know this), it is possible to know by casino location who has higher payout machines. Casinos must report this data to local or state gaming regulatory agencies and they in turn release this information to the public. *Casino Player* and *Atlantic City* magazines for example report the slot machine payout percentages on a monthly basis.

In the old days, casino managers placed the higher payout machines near the entrances to the casino to attract other players who constantly heard the clanking of coins. Nowadays the tendency is to place the higher payout machines in carousels at the end of the isles.

Slots Popularity

Slot machines have become more technical with microchips and video displays. Their popularity continues to grow to the point that casinos usually devote about half of their floor space to slots and the rest to table games. The limits on slot machines have also increased and it's not uncommon to find $25, $100, even $500 slot machines (yes that's $500 per pull).

Slot Clubs

Slot clubs reward players who frequently play slot machines. It's the same concept that airlines use (frequent flyers) except slot players are rewarded with gifts, special invitations to shows and parties, free or discounted rooms and other amenities. Players can join a slot club by simply applying. They are issued a slot club card (like a credit card) which they insert into a special card reader on the machine. These machines will record the amount of money the player puts into the machine. The more money played over time, the greater will be the rewards. Ask any casino for literature that describes their slot club program.

Recommendation

Your best bet is a high payback dollar machine (97-99%). If you play the progressives, always insert the maximum coins. And always read the instructions on each machine so you understand the payoffs. Most new machines for example do not pay off in coins on each win but rather give the player credit which is visible on the display. To receive your credit in coins a player must depress the cash out button. If you play slots regularly, by all means join a slot club. At least you'll be getting back part of the money you invested in freebies. Slots are tough to beat and the key is to quit ahead if you're lucky to hit a few jackpots. Try this simple money management system the next time you play the slots:

1. Buy a roll of coins with an amount of money that you can afford to lose should the worse happen.

2. Put the coins in a slot cup. These coins are your playing bankroll.

3. Play all of your coins into a machine making sure you don't combine any winnings with your playing bankroll.

4. After you have played all the coins in your cup, count up the coins in the slot pan (or check the credit meter).

5. If you have less coins than you started with you are obviously behind. Put the coins back into the slot cup and use this new playing bankroll to repeat the process at a different machine.

6. If you have more coins in the pan than you started with, you're obviously ahead. Take your original bankroll plus 10% (1 out of 10 coins) of your profit and pocket it! Put the remaining coins back into the slot cup and repeat the process. At this point you've got your original bankroll plus a little profit locked up and you are now playing with your winnings.

7. After you have played your winnings, add up the coins in the pan (or check the credit meter) and pocket half of them. The other half can go back into the slot cup and the process repeated.

8. Continue this process until you run out of coins - but don't fret, because at this point you have your original bankroll plus profit socked away.

Many slot machines allow a player to insert a dollar (or higher) bills into a bill acceptor at the machine and then the machine will register the amount in credits. Players can use these credits to play and any winnings are added back to the credits. You can still use the above money management playing system on machines that allow credit. In fact it is even easier since the machine in essence does all the accounting for you automatically. Just stay with the basic concept of pocketing your minibank and some of your profits and you will be surprised at how many more times you will walk away from those machines a winner.

Slot Teams

In recent years, sophisticated slot players have pooled their bankrolls and formed slot teams. They track the amount of progressive jackpots throughout an area and when a specific jackpot gets to a certain level they dispatch teams of players to these machines. They will typically play non-stop until a jackpot is hit or they go broke. However, when they hit a jackpot they usually leave which is why team players are usually frowned upon by casino bosses. The key to team play is to determine the theoretical hit point at which it pays to play than go all out hoping you hit before your bankroll is consumed.

11

POKER

Objective

To win the money in the pot by either having the best poker hand or by forcing all other players out of the game.

Types of Poker

The most popular games played in casinos are seven card stud, hold 'em and draw poker. In the majority of games, the high poker hand wins. However in one popular game, lowball, the lowest hand wins. New versions of poker, noteably, Caribbean Stud and Let It Ride, have gained in popularity.

Hand Rankings

In games in which the high hand wins, the royal flush is the highest hand and a hand without a pair is the lowest. The ranking of hands is as follows:

Royal flush	(A, K, Q, J, 10 in one suit)
Straight flush	(Five consecutive cards in one suit)
4-of-a-kind	(Four cards of same rank)
Full house	(Three of a kind with a pair)
Flush	(Five cards of the same suit)
Straight	(Five consecutive cards but not of same suit)
3-of-a-kind	(Three cards of same rank)
2 Pair	(Two separate pairs of identically ranked cards)
One Pair	(One pair of identically ranked cards)
No pair	(A hand with five odd cards)

In lowball poker, the ace counts as one and the lowest hand is 5, 4, 3, 2, A. (In low poker, straights and flushes don't count). The next lowest hand is 6, 4, 3, 2, A, followed by 6, 5, 3, 2, A. Normally you call out the two highest cards in your hand, for example a 6, 5 in the latter hand.

Dealing
In casinos there is a house dealer who deals the cards. A button moves around the table clockwise and the player to the left of the button must bet first.

Antes
Prior to the start of each game, players must place chips in the center of the table. This is known as an ante. The amount of the ante varies but it is usually a small percentage of the average bet.

Betting Limits
Normally, the casinos will set betting limits for each table and game. Signs are usually posted indicating the limits. Usually the higher limit is twice the smaller limit (eg $1-2 or $5-10), however sometimes there is a higher spread (e.g. $1-5).

In a $5-10 game, all bets before the draw (including any raises) are $5 and increments of $5. After the draw, a player may wager $10 and increments of $10 when raising.

Chips are used in casinos at poker tables. You purchase your chips at the time you buy-in (exchange cash for chips). As a rule of thumb you should buy-in for 40 to 50 times the minimum bet. This is known as your table stake. You can always exchange additional cash for chips between deals but if you're involved in a game, you can only use your existing table stake for betting purposes.

Options

In poker a player has several options. Players may either bet or pass (or check). The latter means the player does not want to make a bet but is still in the game. A player may also decide to fold or throw his cards in and get out of the game. Players may also call (bet the same as previous bet) or raise the bet. Usually there is a limit of three raises in any one round. Checking then raising is usually permitted (not usually the case in private games).

Rake

The casino makes its profit at poker by keeping a small percentage of each pot. This is known as the rake and the amount taken usually varies from one casino to another. Normally the rake is 5% of the pot and sometimes there is a limit on the amount of the rake. There should be a posted sign indicating the rake. If not ask the dealer or supervisor.

Seven Card Stud

In this popular form of poker, each player receives two face down cards, then four face up followed by the final card which is dealt face down. The ante is usually 10% of the minimum bet. The cards are dealt one at a time to each player. After every player receives the initial two face down cards and third face up card, the first round of betting occurs. This first round of betting is known as Third Street. The player with the lowest card on the table starts the betting. If two (or more) players have the same low card, then the card suit determines who bets first in this order - clubs (first), then diamonds, hearts and finally spades. Each player in turn (clockwise) must then either call (equal the bet), raise the bet, or fold. When the betting is completed the dealer deals another round of cards face-up to each player (Fourth Street). The player with the highest hand showing bets first. All other players follow (similar to Third Street). This sequence of betting continues with Fifth and Sixth Street. When a pair shows or its Fifth Street, a player can usually bet the high limit (eg. if its a $5-10 game, $10 can be bet). The last card, Seventh Street, is dealt face down. A final round of betting occurs followed by the showdown or revealing the hands. The highest hand wins the pot.

Recommendation

As a general guide, limit your play to those games that have a 5% (no higher) rake and a dollar limit on the rake. Fold on Third Street unless you have at least a pair and if the pair is low, you should also have an ace, king or queen odd card. If you don't improve your three card flush or straight by Fourth Street, fold. If someone else has a higher pair then yours, fold unless you also have an odd card higher in rank than the high pair. When you have a good hand, play aggressively and raise especially if you have everyone else beat on the table. Don't stay in and chase other players - only the highest hand wins not second best.

Texas Hold 'Em

In this game of poker, the casino dealer deals out two cards face down one at a time to each player. The first player to receive a card is the player to the left of the button (ie the player with the button gets the last card). After all players receive their two cards, there is a round of betting where players can either call, raise, or fold. Checking is not allowed on this round (this first round of betting is called the blind). The dealer now deals three cards face up in the center of the table (these cards are called the flop). Another round of betting commences. The dealer places a fourth card face-up on the table (Fourth Street) followed by another round of betting. Finally, the fifth and last card is placed by the dealer face-up in the middle of the table followed by the final round of betting (Fifth Street). Players choose their best five-card hand among seven cards - the two initial cards dealt face-down and the five community cards in the middle of the layout. The winner is the player with the highest poker hand.

Recommendation

You should continue to play without hesitation if your first two cards dealt to you are A-A, K-K, Q-Q and A-K or A-Q suited. Other playable hands are any two cards higher than 10 such as K-J. Never stay in if you have a pair less than 7's. If you have a pair of 7's through J's, these are usually weak hands and seldom should you stay in.

You generally want to see all lower cards in the flop than the rank of your pair. Bet aggressively if you have a strong hand to force players out before the flop. Your best position on the table is to bet last which justifies staying-in with marginal hands (as long as the betting hasn't escalated). Finally, observe the play of your opponents to determine who tends to stay in with weak hands and who stays with only strong hands.

Draw Poker - Jacks or Better

In this game, all player's cards are unseen. The ante is usually 10% of the maximum bet. The casino dealer deals five cards face down one at a time to each player. The player to the left of the button acts first. A round of betting occurs prior to the draw. A player must have at least a pair of jacks or better to start the betting. If a player does not have at least a pair of jacks, the player must check. After a player starts the betting (or opens), each player in turn in a clockwise manner can either call, raise or fold. Once this initial round of betting is complete, players may discard as many cards as they wish and receive new cards. Another round of betting occurs followed by the show of the hands. The highest poker hand wins the pot.

Recommendation

Your playing position is very important in draw poker. If you are one of the first to bet (eg. first three players out of eight), you are very vulnerable and therefore as a guideline, don't open with less than a pair of aces or kings. If you are in position 4, 5, 6 (middle), don't open unless you have at least a pair of queens, and if you are in the best position (7, 8), only open with at least a pair of jacks. Do not open with two small pairs unless you bet in position 7 or 8. Plan on raising if you hold a strong hand going into the draw (eg. pair of aces, kings). As in Hold'em, study your opposition to learn who plays conservatively and who plays more aggressively.

Draw Poker Lowball

Lowball poker is the opposite of high poker. The lowest hand is 5, 4, 3, 2, A (straights and flushes don't count and the ace counts as 1). Lowball poker is generally played with an ante. Each player receives five cards one at a time face down. Player to the left of the button is designated as the blind and bets first. This player must make a bet on this round no matter what the value of his or her hand. After the blind bets, each player in a clockwise manner may either raise, call or fold. Checking is not allowed on this level. Each player may then draw as many cards as they wish, another round of betting occurs and then the hands are revealed. The player with the lowest hand wins the pot.

Recommendation

Always remember that any hand with five odd cards beats a hand with a pair. The highest ranking card in an odd hand determines the strength of the hand. The best hand is 5, 4, 3, 2, ace, a so called five high hand. Five, six and seven high hands are strong hands. Never stay in if you have to draw two cards. You should stand with your initial five cards (called staying pat) if your high card is at least an 8 (betting early) or 9, 10, if betting later. If you need to draw one card, you should have at least four cards with 7 as high (betting early) or 8, 9 high card (betting later). Always play your pat hands aggressively by raising.

Caribbean Stud

This form of poker is very popular in the Caribbean casinos and on cruise ships and it recently has been introduced into casinos in this country. Unlike regular poker where players compete against each other, in Caribbean stud players compete against the house. The game is played on a blackjack size table and every player must ante up prior to the deal. There is also an optional wager that each player can make to be eligible for a special jackpot. This bet is one dollar and players who wish to make this bet place a dollar chip in the chip-slot in front of them. A progressive meter located on the table indicates the amount of the jackpot. As more players make the jackpot wager, the jackpot increases (it usually starts at $10,000 and then grows).

All players who ante are given five cards facedown by the dealer. The dealer receives four cards down and one up. Players look at these cards then decide whether to make a wager (or call), which must be twice the ante, or fold and forfeit the ante to the dealer.

The dealer reveals his or her four downcards. If the dealer does *not* have at least an ace, king, the players receive a 1 to 1 payoff on their ante and all bet wagers are returned to the player. If instead the dealer has an ace, king (or higher), the dealer will compare his or her hand to each player's hand. If the dealer's cards beat the player's cards, the dealer collects the player's ante and wager bet. If the dealer and player's hand are identical, no money is exchanged (tie). If the player's hand beats the dealer's hand, the player receives even money on his ante bet and a bonus payoff for the wager bet. The normal bonus payoffs are as follows:

Ace-King	1 to 1
One pair	1 to 1
Two pair	2 to 1
3-of-a-kind	3 to 1
Straight	4 to 1
Flush	5 to 1
Full house	7 to 1
4-of-a-kind	20 to 1
Straight flush	50 to 1
Royal flush	100 to 1

The only limit on the payouts is the table limit.

The progressive jackpot is a totally independent process and the normal jackpot payoffs are as follows:

Royal flush	100% of jackpot
Straight flush	10% of jackpot
4-of-a-kind	$100
Full house	$75
Flush	$50

Keep in mind that to win the above progressive jackpot, a player must have placed one dollar in the jackpot chip-slot.

The above payoffs may vary from casino to casino, check the posted rules or ask the dealer or supervisor.

Basic Playing Strategy

The following simple basic playing strategy will cut the casino's edge to about 5.3%.

• If you hold a pair or higher, then make the extra wager.

- If you hold Ace-King plus another card which equals the dealer's upcard than make the extra wager.
- If you don't have either of the above, fold.

Recommendation

The average payback is about 95%, making it not as good a deal as regular poker. The progressive jackpot is not recommended unless the jackpot grows to $265,000 or higher. In general, play Caribbean stud poker for fun with small stakes. Do your serious poker playing at the regular poker tables.

Let It Ride

Let It Ride is a relatively new casino table game that has grown in popularity in casinos throughout the country. It was developed by Shuffle Master, Inc., the folks that invented the automatic shuffling machines that you now see being used at blackjack tables, caribbean stud tables, and of course the Let It Ride tables.

What makes the game so appealing to players is that they can remove up to two of three initial bets it they don't think they can win. Kind of a unique rule when you think about it. Where else, other than surrender in blackjack, can you remove part of your bet when the odds are stacked against you.

Actually, the game is easy to play which is another reason for its popularity. It is based on the all-American game of poker which is familiar to most casino players. Unlike the regular table game of poker where players compete against each other, with Let It Ride players play against the house.

The rules are easy to follow. Prior to the deal each player makes three separate bets of equal amounts in the three betting spaces in front of each player (labeled "1", "2" and "$"). Each player and dealer are then dealt three cards face down. The dealer discards one of his cards and the remaining two cards become community cards for all players. There are no draw cards in Let It Ride.

The objective is to end up with at least a pair of tens or higher. Payoffs are scaled based upon the rank of the hand. If a player ends up with a pair of tens for example the payoff is 1 to 1. A full house pays 11 to 1 and a royal flush 1000 to 1.

Each player looks at the three initial cards dealt to them and then must decide to let bet number 1 ride or to take it down. If you want to let the bet ride tuck your cards under your chips in betting spot number 1. If you want the bet returned to you, simply scratch the cards on the table (like hitting in blackjack) and the dealer will return the chips in betting spot number 1 to you. After each player makes their decision, the dealer will face one of the two community cards. Players agains go through the process of either letting their bet in the number 2 spot ride or taking it down. Finally the dealer will face the last community card and inspect each players five cards (the initial three cards plus the two community cards). If your five card hand contains at least a pair of tens or higher you will win the amount listed in the payoff schedule for each bet you let ride.

Obviously you should let your first and second bet ride if you have a pair of tens, picture cards, or aces. Let the second bet ride when your four card hand has a potential for a big payoff such as a four card straight, flush, or royal flush.

The casino's edge is about 3.5% but you will lose at a higher rate unless you catch a big payoff hand. Overall about 70% of the hands dealt to you will be less than a pair of tens (you will lose). So unless you get lucky and are dealt a high payoff hand, most likely your bankroll will slowly dwindle. But if you do get lucky and are dealt a straight or higher, instead of letting it ride on the next hand, be smart, take down your chips, and run to the cashier with your profits.

Recently there have been Let It Ride Tournaments with jackpots up to $3 million. To enter you must make an additional one dollar side bet in each hand and hope you are one of the lucky players that end up with the highest poker hand over a specified playing period. These players from across the country are assembled at one casino location for the finals which feature the million dollar prizes.

"Poker is one of the most fascinating gambling games, because it combines three elements: skill, luck, and psychology. It is this combination which draws millions of players to card tables around America."

J. Edward Allen

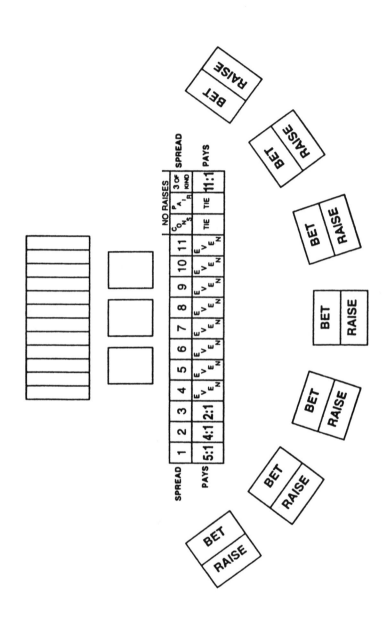

12

RED DOG

Objective

To guess if the value of a random selected card is between the value of two cards.

Card Values

Any card from 2 to 10 counts face value
Any jack counts as 11
Any queen counts as 12
Any king counts as 13
Any ace counts as 14

Mechanics

The game is played on a table similar to a blackjack table. One or more decks of cards are used. Players make a wager then the dealer places two cards on the table face-up. All players are betting on this same community hand. Depending upon the value of the two cards, players have the option of making a raise wager and a third card may or may not be drawn.

Type of Hands

Pair Hand: When the two cards dealt by the dealer have the same value (e.g. pair of 6's), this is called a pair hand. In this situation, the dealer will automatically draw a third card. If the value of the third card is the same as the original two cards, all players win 11 to 1. If instead the value of the third card is different than the original two cards, the hand is a tie or push (player neither wins nor loses the original wager).

Consecutive Hand: When the value of the initial two cards are consecutive (e.g. 4, 5 or Q, K) this is called a consecutive hand. The dealer does not draw a third card. The hand is a tie or push.

Non-consecutive Hand: Most of the red dog hands fall into this category. When the original two cards are neither a pair nor consecutive, the dealer will announce the spread and place a marker on the layout indicating the spread. The spread is the number of values that fall between the values of the initial two cards. For example if the initial cards were 2 and 8, the spread is 5 because there are five values between 2 and 8 (3, 4, 5, 6, 7).

Whenever a spread is announced, players may make a secondary wager (raise wager) up to the amount of the original wager prior to the dealer dealing the third card.

Players win if the value of the third card is *between* the value of the initial two cards (Note: if it is identical to either of the two initial cards, the bet is lost). There is never a tie in non-consecutive hands.

Payouts on Winning Hands

All winning wagers and raise wagers in non-consecutive hands are paid at payout odds determined by the spread.

Spread	Payout
one	5 to 1
two	4 to 1
three	2 to 1
four thru eleven	1 to 1

Recommended Strategy

The only time you should ever make the raise wager is when the spread is seven or more (only when it's seven or more will you have a better than 50% chance of winning). Red dog is fun to play and usually the stakes are low, however the casino's edge is too high (ca 3.5%) for serious players.

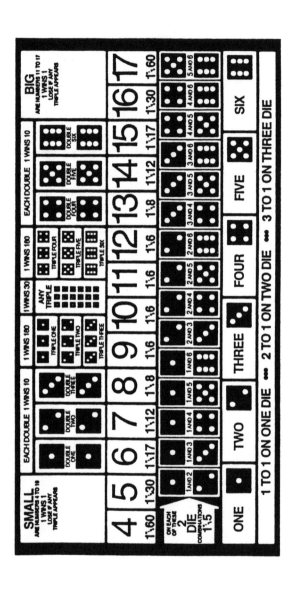

13

SIC BO

Objective

To guess the individual die numbers or combinations of dice numbers that will appear when three dice are rolled.

Mechanics

Players make their wager on the layout. The casino dealer shakes the shaker containing the three dice then removes the cover and announces the total. The dealer enters the numeric value of each die into an electronic device that causes the winning combinations to be illuminated on the layout. Dealer collects all losing wagers and pays off all winning wagers at the posted odds.

Different Types of Bets

There are over 50 possible betting options in sic bo. They are summarized below into single die wagers, two dice wagers and three dice wagers.

1. Single-die wager

(A) **One of a kind** - Player bets that one or more of the three dice shows a numeric value equal to the number wagered. There are six possible die numbers that can be bet: 1, 2, 3, 4, 5 or 6. Winning payoffs are 1 to 1 if the number selected appears on one die, 2 to 1 if the number shows on two dice, and 3 to 1 if it appears on all three dice.

2. Two-dice wagers

(B) **Two of a kind** - Player bets that the same number appears on two of the three dice. You can wager on either two 1s, 2s, 3s, 4s, 5s or 6s. Winning payoff is 8 to 1.

(C) **Any two-dice combinations** - Player bets that a combination of two specific but different numeric values appear on at least two of the dice. There are 15 different two-dice numeric values, which are summarized on the layout. The first betting box shows the numbers 1 and 2. To win, the numbers of at least two of three dice must be 1 and 2. The winning payoff for these wagers is 5 to 1.

3. Three-dice wagers

(D) **Three of a kind** - Player bets that the same number appears on all three dice. You can wager on either three 1s, 2s, 3s, 4s, 5s or 6s. Winning payoff is 150 to 1, a long-shot bet with a high payoff.

(E) **Any three of a kind** - Player bets that any of the numbers 1 through 6 will appear on all three dice. Thus if three 1s, 2s, 3s, 4s, 5s or 6s appear on the three dice, you win this bet. Winning payoff is 24 to 1.

(F) **Total value bet** - Player bets on the numerical total of the three dice. The totals that the player can wager are 4 through 17. Thus if a player wagers on the total 10 and numbers of the three dice are 4, 3, 3 (adding up to 10), the player wins. The payoffs for the total value bets vary depending upon the total and are as follows:

Total	Payoff
4,17	50 to 1
5,16	18 to 1
6,15	14 to 1
7,14	12 to 1
8,13	8 to 1
9,12	6 to 1

(G) **Small bet** - Players bet that the numeric total of all three dice equals any one of the following totals: 4, 5, 6, 7, 8, 9 or 10. (note: bet loses if three of a kind appear). Winning payoff is even money (1 to 1).

(H) **Big bet** - Player bets that the numeric total of all three dice equals any of the following totals: 11, 12, 13, 14, 15, 16 or 17 (note: bet loses if three of a kind appear). Winning payoff is even money (1 to 1).

Casino Advantage

Since three dice are used in sic bo, there is the possibility of 216 (6x6x6) combinations that will give 16 different totals ranging from 3 (when 1 appears on each die) up to 18 (6 appears on each die). By comparing the true odds of rolling any combination with the winning payoff, it is quite easy to calculate the casino advantage for each bet. This is summarized in the table on the next page.

Wager	Payoff	Casino Advantage (Percent)
SINGLE DIE:		
One of a Kind	1 to 1 (one die)	7.87
	2 to 1 (two dice)	
	3 to 1 (three dice)	
TWO DICE:		
Two of a kind	8 to 1	37.5
Any two dice		
combination	5 to 1	16.7
THREE DICE:		
Three of a kind	150 to 1	30.1
Any three of a kind	24 to 1	30.6
TOTAL VALUE BET:		
4,17	50 to 1	29.2
5,16	18 to 1	47.2
6,15	14 to 1	30.6
7,14	12 to 1	9.7
8,13	8 to 1	12.5
9,12	6 to 1	19.0
10,11	6 to 1	12.5
SMALL BET	1 to 1	2.8
BIG BET	1 to 1	2.8

Casino Snafu

Is it possible to beat the casino at sic bo? No, but several astute players gave one of the new Mississippi casinos a run for its money. The casino had mistakenly listed the payoffs on the layout for the three dice total of 4 and 17 at 80 to 1 instead of 50 to 1. As a result, players who bet on the 4 and 17 actually had a 12.5%

edge over the casino! Professional players were betting the maximum allowed and cashed in big time until the casino discovered its mistake and shut down the table. Historically, it was one of the biggest money-making opportunities for those casino players who were smart enough to discover and take advantage of the error.

Recommendation

Your best bet is the big or small wager that pays 1 to 1 (casino advantage is 2.8%). Do not be tempted by the high payoff wagers as the casino's advantage is much too high.

Mark Price Here

1	2	3	4	5	6	7	8	9	10
11	12	13	14	15	16	17	18	19	20
21	22	23	24	25	26	27	28	29	30
31	32	33	34	35	36	37	38	39	40
41	42	43	44	45	46	47	48	49	50
51	52	53	54	55	56	57	58	59	60
61	62	63	64	65	66	67	68	69	70
71	72	73	74	75	76	77	78	79	80

KENO RUNNERS ARE AVAILABLE FOR YOUR CONVENIENCE
WE ARE NOT RESPONSIBLE IF TICKETS ARE TOO LATE FOR CURRENT GAME

WINNING TICKETS PAID IMMEDIATELY AFTER EACH KENO GAME

14

KENO

Objective
The objective of the game is for the player to guess which numbers from 1 to 80 will be randomly selected by a computer or machine.

Mechanics
Keno is played in an area of the casino known as keno lounges or parlors. The winning numbers for each game are electronically displayed on keno boards located throughout the casino including restaurants.

Players select which numbers they believe will be drawn using a keno ticket. These tickets look like a bingo ticket except it contains the number 1 thru 80 in eight rows of ten numbers.

Players mark whatever number or combination of numbers they think will be selected by crossing out the numbers on the keno ticket with a crayon or pen. There are literally billions of different combinations of numbers but the simplest tickets are known as spot tickets, in which the player marks specific numbers. For example if a player marks numbers 7 and 20, this is known as a two spot ticket. A player who marks 3, 10, 12, 20, 50, 60 is playing a six spot ticket.

Once you've marked your numbers on the ticket you should indicate the amount you wish to bet on the top right corner of the ticket. One to two dollar minimum bet keno games are readily available but of course players could wager more if they choose. Once you've completed marking your keno ticket you turn in your ticket with bet to any one of the keno writers or keno runners located throughout the casino and in restaurants. The keno runners will handle making your bet and return to you the authorized copy of your keno ticket. This ticket will contain the number of the next drawing. If you win, the keno runners will also pick up your winnings and return them to you (it is customary to tip the runners for this service).

At the start of each keno game, the game number will appear on the keno board and then one by one the 20 winning numbers will be lit (there are 80 numbers and in each game, twenty are selected). If you have marked some of the winning keno numbers on your keno ticket, you win. The number of matches required for a win and the corresponding payoffs depend upon how many numbers you selected and how much you bet.

Every casino provides players with brochures that explain the payoffs for each type of ticket as well as the types of bets allowed.

High Payoffs

Keno offers players of modest means an opportunity to win up to $50,000 (and more in some casinos that have progressive jackpots) for only a modest bet of $2 or less. It also takes little effort to play.

Casino Edge

The casino edge in keno is very high. For example, the casinos pay 2 to 1 on a one spot ticket yet the odds of winning are 3 to 1 (60 numbers not selected to 20 that are). With a 2 to 1 payback on a 3 to 1 bet, the casino's edge or advantage is a whopping 25%! Depending upon how many numbers are marked and the corresponding payoff, it is feasible to calculate the casino's edge for every type of bet. When doing this exercise, for most keno games, the calculations show a casino edge that is usually much greater than the normal table games and even slot machines (some keno tickets have a casino edge of 50 to 60%).

Recommendation
Play keno for fun but not for serious gambling.

Summary of Keno Bets

Straight Ticket. Player marks from one to the maximum number of spots allowed by the casino.

Split Ticket. Allows a player to write two or more straight tickets at one time on one ticket. A player marks two or more groups of numbers separate from each other. The common method of separating the two groups of numbers is to either circle each group or draw a line between them. A player who circles two groups of five numbers on one ticket indicates this in the margin by writing the fraction 2/5.

Way Ticket. This is a keno ticket marked with at least three equal groups of numbers and each group is combined with the other groups, to form several straight ticket combinations. For example a player marking and circling the group 1,2,3,4,5 and the group 31,32,33,34,35 and finally the group 71,72,73,74,75 means he is betting on each group plus the combination of the first and second group (making a 10 spot group) plus the combination of the first and third group (another 10 spot) and finally the second and third group (another 10 spot group). A player marking his ticket in this manner writes in the margin 3/10 (three groupings of 10 numbers).

Combination Ticket. This is a ticket in which the player selects at least two groups of any number of spots and selects how the groups are to be combined to form multiple tickets within one ticket. Thus, for example, a player can mark three groups of four spots and circle each group. By writing in the margin 3/8 and also 1/12 you indicate that you want to combine the three eight spot with one twelve spot. This is a simple combination ticket of three eight spots and one twelve spots.

King Ticket. With this ticket, one number is circled by itself and used in combination with other circled groups. For example if a player circled the number 7 and two and three group of numbers, the game can be played as a 3 spot (king plus two spot), 4 spot (king and 3 spot), 5 spot (2 spot and 3 spot), and a 6 spot (king plus 2 and 3 spot). You would write in the margin the fractions 1/3, 1/4, 1/5, and 1/6.

Muti Race Ticket. This is a keno ticket wagered for more than one game. All of the games covered by the ticket must be consecutive and must be wagered at the same amount.

"The trick (to getting more than your share of comps) is to make it appear that you're betting more, playing longer, and playing worse than you really are."

Max Rubin

15

CASINO FREEBIES

A fair amount of questions that I receive from players has to do with comps. For those unfamiliar with the term, a comp is short for complimentary, and it is a way for the casinos to give back to the player something of value for risking their money at the tables or slots. A comp might be a free meal or discounted or free lodging or even free transportation. In general the higher your bankroll and betting limits the higher the value of the comp.

So how do the casinos know how much to give back to the player? And how does a player get his comp? Read on. You will learn the basics of comps.

The casinos use a simple equation to rate a player who plays blackjack, for example. This rating determines how much the casino can expect to win from that player. Based on this calculated expected win, the casinos will usually give back to the player anywhere from 25% to 50% as a comp.

The equation that the casinos use to determine the comp amount is:

Average bet size times number of hands per hour times number of hours played times casino's edge times 40 per cent.

Suppose you play blackjack with an average bet size of $10. Sometimes you will bet more and sometimes less but overall you'll average about $10 per hand. Suppose also that you play blackjack at your favorite casino for 4 hours. In general you will be dealt 60 hands per hour when you play blackjack. The latter of course varies depending upon how many players there are at the table, how fast the dealer deals the cards and how often the dealer shuffles. But 60 hands per hour is a good approximation.

The next part of the comp equation asks for the casinos edge or advantage. For blackjack, most casinos use 2 per cent as their average edge against the masses of individuals who play blackjack. If you are a skilled blackjack player the casinos edge would be lower. Likewise if you are a novice and know very little about the basic playing strategy the casino's edge would be higher.

Finally you'll notice the 40% in the equation. This is the average per cent rebate the casinos will give back to a player based upon his or her expected loss.

If you do the arithmetic the casinos expect to win $48 from our blackjack player ($10 average bet size times 4 hours times 60 hands per hour times 2% casino edge). The casinos are willing to give back 40% of their expected $48 win or $19 in comps.

How does a player get his $19 comp? Simply ask the floor supervisor. In most cases in this example the player would be given a comp for a meal in a casino restaurant or buffet.

Here are some tips for getting the most from the casino's comping policies. You'll get the most returns if you play blackjack skillfully. Why? Because the casinos assume they have a 2% edge against blackjack players. In fact if you learn the basic playing strategy, the casinos actual edge is only about 0.5%. This means in our example above, the players expected loss is a lot less than $48 (actually $12). The smart blackjack player is actually getting $19 worth of comps for an expected loss of only $12. Get the picture?

Comps are not always automatic. The floor supervisor has

the freedom to give a comp as they wish (known as the power of the pen). If they are having a bad day, they are usually not too liberal giving out comps. But as a general rule, women will usually have an easier time getting a comp especially from a male supervisor. I've tested this with my wife and believe me after 25 years she usually will get a comp a lot easier than I (in most cases she can play for less time or lower stakes and get an equivalent comp as I can betting more and longer).

It's also important to check out the casino's comping policies. Don't expect much in the way of comps from say a Caesar's Palace casino unless you bet at high levels. Casinos that cater more to the average or low end player will be much more liberal in their comping policies. The easiest way to find this out is to call the casino's marketing department and ask about their comp policies.

One final caution - I've seen too many players betting over their limits just to get a comp. The name of the game is to get your fair share of comps at the level of betting which you feel comfortable with. Do not, I repeat, do not overbet just for the sake of getting a comp!

If you want to learn more about comps, I can recommend Max Rubin's *Comp City*. Although it contains some controversial advise for getting comps, overall it is the best book on the market explaining what use to be a very secretive part of the casino business.

"When the gambling tournament advertising brochures proclaim, 'Anyone can win,' believe it. Anyone can win."

Haven Earle Haley

16

GAMBLING TOURNAMENTS

Casinos offer gambling tournaments on a regular basis. Players enjoy these tournaments because of the excitement of the competition and the fact that most tournaments offer very large cash prizes. How large you ask? Recently a woman from California won a cool one million dollars in a national slot tournament sponsored by Harrahs Casinos. And not to be outdone, the folks that invented Let It Ride, the popular new table game, gave a three million dollar prize in one of their tournaments.

The most popular tournaments are those involving blackjack, craps, slots, and baccarat. However, from time to time casinos offer tournaments on video poker, table poker, keno, roulette, and other casino games.

Although the rules may vary from one tournament to another, the basic concept of tournaments is simple to understand. All contestants start with the same playing bankroll. Your objective is to end up your playing session with more money than your fellow competitors. It doesn't make a difference whether you end up $5,000 ahead or $1. The player with the most cash wins.

In table games like blackjack, all contestants are assigned

to a specific table and seat. Everyone at your table starts with the same bankroll. After a specified number of hands or set time limit, the player that ends up with the most money advances to the next round to play other table winners. Eventually the field of contestants are whittled down to a final group of 6 or 7 who play a championship round for the big prize.

Slot tournaments are a little different. Here players are given a specific playing bankroll or machine credits. After a specified number of handle pulls or time period the player with the most credits (or winnings) advances to the next round.

The fascination of tournaments are that contestants are competing not only against the casino but also against other players. You try to "beat the dealer" for example in blackjack tournaments but you also must concentrate on the bankrolls of your fellow player so you end up with more money than them.

How you bet in tournaments is the most important factor to improve your chances of winning. Betting strategies employed by your competitors, whether you are ahead or behind the leader, and whether you bet first or last are factors that must be considered before you bet. Knowing when to play it close to protect your bankroll by making small bets and when to let it all out and bet big is crucial in tournament play.

The following tips are based on my experiences of how to get the most from playing in tournaments.

1. Tournament sponsors charge a fee. You should ask how much of the total fees paid by all the contestants will be returned to the players in the form of prizes. Some tournaments return 100% especially the low entry "fun" tournaments where entry fees are as low as $25 or $50. Don't forget to factor in any freebies the sponsoring casinos throw in to contestants. For example I recently played in a tournament in Las Vegas which returned all of the fees in prizes, gave complimentary buffets and show tickets, and offered a discount off the entry fee for a future tournament. Quite a deal!

2. Some tournaments, especially the "fun tournaments" give the players their starting bankroll in non negotiable chips. In other tournaments you must put up your own cash as a starting bankroll. This is where tournament play gets risky because players are betting with their own money.

3. All tournaments have a specific starting bankroll, specific playing rules, a posted minimum and maximum bet, and rules on how players advance. In some tournaments for example, it is only the table winner that advances, in others the top two winners advance. Make sure you read and understand all the rules before entering (sponsors will provide this, just ask).

4. If you lose all your chips in a table game tournament, you are eliminated. Some tournaments allow you to reenter (for another fee). You should always try to end a round with at least one red chip. Don't laugh. I've been in and observed tournaments in which a player has won a round because he had one chip left while everyone else bet it all on the last hand or dice throw and lost.

5. In table game tournaments all players take turns betting first. You have an edge if you bet last because you get to see how much your opponents have bet in relation to their bankroll.

6. Some tournament players bet conservatively from start to end while others make large bets from the get go. From my experiences you need to take a more risky betting style than you would normally. Specifically if you are serious about winning the top prize then you should be prepared to make large bets up to the maximum allowed (usually $500) if that is what it will take to stay ahead or catch the leader. My advice is to bet big until you get the lead then drop back, bet small, and let your opponents try to catch you. If someone passes you, then you need to increase your betting level again until you get the lead, then bet small. Be prepared, however, to bet big, on the last hand or dice throw.

7. You need to learn how to estimate what a stack of chips are worth since it is important you have some idea on the status of the bankrolls of your fellow players. I once witnessed a tournament blackjack player take a ruler and start measuring the height of the stack of chips his opponents had (which by the way, one stack of 10 casino chips measures about one and one quarter inches). Remember it is important to keep track of your opponents bankroll especially the leader so you can adjust your bet size.

8. Be careful of players who take the lead then mimic every bet you make so you have no chance of catching up. This strategy often occurs in craps or baccarat tournaments. For example if a player had the lead in a craps tournament and his closest competitor makes a $300 bet on the pass line, the leader will often do the same. By betting in this manner no one can catch him. On the other hand one way to catch a leader is to bet the opposite of him. If he is betting the pass line, you should bet don't pass. This way if he loses you win. Also be careful in craps tournaments that it is possible for someone to catch you in one or two dice throws by making bets that payoff large amounts (especially the proposition bets). The same goes for the tie bet in baccarat.

9. With slot tournaments, the key is to get as many "spins" of the reels as feasible during the allotted round. This means you must keep your finger(s) constantly tapping on the spin button. I have seen players become distracted during slot tournaments and let precious seconds go by without activating the spin button. Your finger(s) will get tired so you need to learn which jackpots are long enough to allow you to stop and rest a few seconds while the machine totals the winnings in credits.

10. Be careful of unorthodox plays especially in the last hand or dice throw as desperate players do what's necessary to overcome a leader. I once learned this lesson the hard way in the very first blackjack tournament held in Atlantic City. I had the lead going into the last hand. My closest opponent was dealt a blackjack hand

and I knew even with a 3 to 2 payoff on his bet that I had him beat even if he won the hand and I lost. Can you imagine my shock when he doubled down on his ace, ten hand. He drew a picture card for a three card twenty one and won the hand when the dealer busted. He also ended up with $30 more than me and won the semifinal round. (By the way don't think of trying this strategy - doubling on a blackjack hand is no longer allowed).

If you want to get your feet wet in tournaments I would strongly suggest you start in one of the low stakes fun tournaments to see what it is all about. There are also several good books and computer software programs dealing with tournament strategies and I can recommend the ones written by Stanford Wong.

"No one wants to be a loser. So learn how to be happy with a small win, because even a small win beats losing every time."

John Gallehon

17

Money Management

L earning the correct playing strategies is only half the battle. You are doomed to lose if you are not prepared with a sound money management plan. The following guidelines will maximize your profits and minimize your chances of going broke.

1.   Don't play with "scared" money. Set a maximum amount that you can afford to lose and if you lose that amount, quit playing and go home.

2.   Never increase the bet size on consecutive losses. On consecutive wins, increase your bets in a manner that suits your style of play. I would recommend a simple 50% progression or a 1, 2, 3, 5 progression. For a 50% progression, after you win a bet, make your next bet the same plus 50% more. The progression would look like this for a $5 basic bet: $5, $8, $12, $18, $27, $40, $60, etc. You keep increasing your bet until you lose, then you start again at $5. For the 1, 2, 3, 5 win progression, you increase your bet from 1 unit to 2 units to 3 then to a

maximum of 5 units following consecutive wins. For example, the progression for a $5 basic bet is $5, $10, $15, $25 then back to $5.

After you make the maximum 5 unit bet, win or lose, make your next bet 1 unit. This progression therefore, is more conservative than the 50% progression.

3.   Your playing bankroll for the above win progressions should be 100 units. If your minimum bet is $5, you need a $500 playing bankroll.

4.   Don't bring your entire playing bankroll with you - bring enough for 2 or 3 playing sessions (40 to 60 units). Use 20 units per playing session and quit the session if you lose the 20 or win 10 units. Hence, a $5 player with a $500 playing bankroll would use $100 per playing session and quit if the $100 were lost or $50 won.

5.   Don't ever quit a session in the middle of a winning streak. If you manage to win 10 units, keep playing with the goal of winning another 10 units. As long as you keep winning, keep setting 10 unit winning goals. However, when the tide turns and you begin to lose, quit the session with your profit. Remember, a small profit is better than no profit!

6.   As your playing bankroll increases as you win, then increase your bet size. Likewise, decrease the bet size if your playing bankroll decreases. Always make your minimum wager equal to 1/100th of your playing bankroll using the win progression.

The cardinal sin in casino gaming is to chase your losses which means increasing your bets when you are losing in the hopes your next bet will win it all back. Everyone who gambles in a casino sooner or later will experience losses and how you handle yourself in this situation will determine in the long run whether or not you will be a winner. If you've lost one or two of your playing session bankrolls, the best you can do is call it quits and limit your losses. The casinos will always be there for your next visit and if you follow the playing strategies in this book you'll soon be back on the road to winning.

"The real struggle when you are playing is, in most cases, not between you and the casino, but between you and yourself."

Lyle Stuart

18

PSYCHOLOGY OF GAMBLING

Learning proper playing strategies and sound money management principles is only part of a successful casino gambler's game plan. Having a proper playing attitude is just as important.

The typical attitude of losing gamblers is something like this: They always go to the casinos to have fun and of course, they always expect to lose. They experience an emotional high when playing and are invariably swept up in the exciting casino atmosphere. They always feel obligated to take the free drinks offered by the casino as a way of getting even for their losses. And, of course, when they lose, they always blame it on rotten luck, or poor cards, but the consolation for their losing is "well, I had a good time anyway," attitude.

Now, don't get me wrong, having fun should be your first objective when you gamble. But that doesn't mean you shouldn't try to win.

Keep this thought in mind next time you go to a casino to have some fun. First, when you enter a casino, you are entering a place of business. And like all successful businesses, the casinos are operated by shrewd businessmen whose job is firstly, to keep you playing and happy and secondly, to separate you from your money as quickly and painlessly as possible. To meet these objectives, they create an atmosphere in the casino that can be described as a "Disneyland for adults." No clocks to let you know it's time to leave this utopia, no windows to let you see out to the real world, free drinks at the tables, free lounge shows and plenty of pretty girls to keep you happy and playing.

And what happens to the average gambler when he enters this casino designed excitement? For him, the rewards of winning all of the casino's money far outweigh the risks of losing his meager hundred dollar bankroll. And this exciting atmosphere also makes it so easy for the average player to feel lucky and go for broke at the chance of winning that jackpot.

First and foremost, in order to be a winner, you must learn to control your emotions in the casino. As Lyle Stuart, casino gaming author, puts it: "The real struggle when you are playing is, in most cases, not between you and the casino, but between you and yourself." You will find plenty of temptations to keep you playing and losing, therefore, you must learn to develop a sense of timing or awareness of when to play and, more importantly, when to quit.

In short, you must develop the proper playing attitudes to overcome the psychological barriers created by the casinos to keep you losing and to make it difficult for you to leave the tables with a profit. For example, go to the casinos expecting to win (rather than lose). Granted, there are no guarantees that you will win, but likewise there is no guarantee that you have to lose. Always prepare yourself for those inevitable losing sessions. No matter how skillfully you play, sometimes everything will go wrong. Will you quit and call it a day or will you be like most gamblers and dig in for more cash, hoping the tide will turn? And how many gamblers have the attitude that a small profit is better than no profit or a loss? Not many.

Above all, learn to develop a sense of timing for when to play and when to quit. Playing blackjack, for example, if you are tired or have been drinking will cost your dearly.

These attitudes are not always natural. Most of them take an amount of work before you can feel comfortable playing with discipline. But if you develop these proper playing attitudes and learn proper playing and money management strategies, you will be able to enjoy the fun and excitement of casino gambling with a minimum risk to your bankroll. Isn't it worth the effort?

*You can't be a winner until you
learn to quit a winner!*

19

SUMMARY

To be a winner in a casino, you must make only bets with the lowest casino advantage using a proper betting scheme and money management. Go to the casinos with a proper attitude that you are there to have a good time but you intend to give the casinos a fair fight for their money using all the playing and betting skills available to you. Your biggest advantage is the fact that you can quit playing anytime you want. Therefore, try to discipline yourself to quit a session a winner. Winning a small amount is a lot better than losing or breaking even. Just remember that you can't be a winner until you learn to quit a winner. Good luck and play smart.

Suggested Reading

Blackjack
Fundamentals of Blackjack, by Carlson Chambliss and Thomas Roginski. A concise yet thorough survey of the entire field of blackjack.

Professional Blackjack, by Stanford Wong. The bible for serious card counters.

Basic Blackjack, by Stanford Wong. Presents playing strategies for every conceivable variation in rules.

Blackjack: Take the Money and Run, by Henry J. Tamburin. Covers basic, intermediate, and advanced strategies.

Craps
The Dice Doctor, by Sam Grafstein. Contains basic and more advanced playing techniques.

Beat the Craps Out of the Casinos, by Frank Scoblete. Contains several unique crap systems.

Craps: Take the Money and Run, by Henry J. Tamburin. Contains basics plus increased odds playing and betting system.

Roulette
All About Roulette, by John Gollehan. Contains the basics of the game.

Beating the Wheel, by Russell Barnhart. Explains techniques used by skillfull players to win millions from biased roulette wheels.

Baccarat

Winning Baccarat Strategies, by Henry J. Tamburin and Richard Rahm. Contains basics plus effective card counting systems.

Pai Gow Poker

Optional Strategy for Pai Gow Poker, by Stanford Wong. Contains complete playing strategies for setting hands.

How To Play Pai Gow Poker, by George Allen. Excellent beginners book.

Video Poker

Winning Strategies for Video Poker, by Lenny Frome. Contains a complete optimum strategy for all different forms of video poker.

Video Poker, by Stanford Wong. Shows how it's possible to get the edge over the casino.

Victory at Video Poker, by Frank Scoblete. Basics and winning techniques.

Poker

The Basics of Poker, by J. Edward Allen. Good introduction to poker.

Slansky on Poker, by David Slansky. Good advice for hold'em, draw, and tournament play.

Slot Machines

Break the One Armed Bandits, by Frank Scoblete. Explains basics plus where casinos place their loose and tight machines.

Caribbean Stud Poker

Caribbean Stud Poker, by Stanley Ko. Contains basics plus thorough analysis of the game.

Let It Ride

Mastering the Game of Let It Ride, by Stanley Ko. Contains basics plus thorough analysis of the game.

Let It Ride, by Lenny Frome. Excellent beginners introduction to the game with basic playing strategy.

Other Books

The Las Vegas Adviser Guide to Slot Clubs, by Jeffrey Compton. Explains how to get the most from slot clubs.

1996 American Casino Guide, by Steve Bourie. Comprehensive guide to casinos in all states.

Comp City - A Guide to Free Las Vegas Vacations, by Max Rubin. Unique book that explains how to get the most of comps from the casinos.

Casino Tournament Strategy, by Stanford Wong. Comprehensive tournament strategies.

Newsletters and Magazines

One way to keep up with what's going on in the world of casino gambling is to subscribe to a newsletter or magazine. Here are a few I can recommend (write for sample copy):

Casino Player Magazine,
8025 Black Horse Pike, Suite 470
West Atlantic City, NJ 08232

Midwest Gaming & Travel Magazine
409 Tenth Street S.E., Suite 100, Waseca, MN 56093

Blackjack Confidential Magazine
P.O. Box 8087 Cherry Hill, NJ 08002-0087

Las Vegas Advisor
3687 S. Procyon Ave, Las Vegas, NV 89103

Blackjack Forum
414 Santa Clara Ave, Oakland, CA 94610

Blackjack Review
P.O. Box 541907, Merritt Island, FL 32954-1967

Current Blackjack News
7910 Ivanhoe #34, LaJolla, CA 92037-4511

A complete catalog containing the above plus hundreds of additional books, software, and videos on gambling can be obtained from these sources:

Gamblers Book Club, Las Vegas 1-800-634-6243
Gamblers General Store, Las Vegas 1-800-332-2447

APPENDIX I

BLACKJACK BASIC

STRATEGY CHARTS

138

Chart 1
Multiple Deck Basic Strategy
Dealer stands on soft 17
Doubling on any two cards
Doubling after pair splitting permitted

Dealer's Upcard

Your Hand	2	3	4	5	6	7	8	9	10	A
17	S	S	S	S	S	S	S	S	S	S
16	S	S	S	S	S	H	H	H*	H*	H*
15	S	S	S	S	S	H	H	H	H*	H
14	S	S	S	S	S	H	H	H	H	H
13	S	S	S	S	S	H	H	H	H	H
12	H	H	S	S	S	H	H	H	H	H
11	D	D	D	D	D	D	D	D	D	H
10	D	D	D	D	D	D	D	D	H	H
9	H	D	D	D	D	H	H	H	H	H
8	H	H	H	H	H	H	H	H	H	H
A,8	S	S	S	S	S	S	S	S	S	S
A,7	S	D	D	D	D	S	S	H	H	H
A,6	H	D	D	D	D	H	H	H	H	H
A,5	H	H	D	D	D	H	H	H	H	H
A,4	H	H	D	D	D	H	H	H	H	H
A,3	H	H	H	D	D	H	H	H	H	H
A,2	H	H	H	D	D	H	H	H	H	H
A,A	P	P	P	P	P	P	P	P	P	P
10,10	S	S	S	S	S	S	S	S	S	S
9,9	P	P	P	P	P	S	P	P	S	S
8,8	P	P	P	P	P	P	P	P	P	P
7,7	P	P	P	P	P	P	H	H	H	H
6,6	P	P	P	P	P	H	H	H	H	H
5,5	Always Treat as 10, never Split									
4,4	H	H	H	P	P	H	H	H	H	H
3,3	P	P	P	P	P	P	H	H	H	H
2,2	P	P	P	P	P	P	H	H	H	H

*Surrender if offered
S= STAND   H= HIT   D= DOUBLE   P= SPLIT

Chart 2 139

Multiple Deck Basic Strategy
Dealer stands on soft 17
Doubling on any two cards
Doubling after pair splitting *not* permitted

Your Hand	Dealer's Upcard									
	2	3	4	5	6	7	8	9	10	A
17	S	S	S	S	S	S	S	S	S	S
16	S	S	S	S	S	H	H	H*	H*	H*
15	S	S	S	S	S	H	H	H	H*	H
14	S	S	S	S	S	H	H	H	H	H
13	S	S	S	S	S	H	H	H	H	H
12	H	H	S	S	S	H	H	H	H	H
11	D	D	D	D	D	D	D	D	D	H
10	D	D	D	D	D	D	D	D	H	H
9	H	D	D	D	D	H	H	H	H	H
8	H	H	H	H	H	H	H	H	H	H
A,8	S	S	S	S	S	S	S	S	S	S
A,7	S	D	D	D	D	S	S	H	H	H
A,6	H	D	D	D	D	H	H	H	H	H
A,5	H	H	D	D	D	H	H	H	H	H
A,4	H	H	D	D	D	H	H	H	H	H
A,3	H	H	H	D	D	H	H	H	H	H
A,2	H	H	H	D	D	H	H	H	H	H
A,A	P	P	P	P	P	P	P	P	P	P
10,10	S	S	S	S	S	S	S	S	S	S
9,9	P	P	P	P	P	S	P	P	S	S
8,8	P	P	P	P	P	P	P	P	P	P
7,7	P	P	P	P	P	P	H	H	H	H
6,6	H	P	P	P	P	H	H	H	H	H
5,5	Always Treat as 10, never Split									
4,4	H	H	H	H	H	H	H	H	H	H
3,3	H	H	P	P	P	P	H	H	H	H
2,2	H	H	P	P	P	P	H	H	H	H

*Surrender if offered
S= STAND   H= HIT   D= DOUBLE   P=SPLIT

Chart 3

Multiple Deck Basic Strategy
Dealer stands on soft 17
Doubling only on 10 and 11
Doubling after pair splitting *not* permitted

Dealer's Upcard

Your Hand	2	3	4	5	6	7	8	9	10	A
17	S	S	S	S	S	S	S	S	S	S
16	S	S	S	S	S	H	H	H*	H*	H*
15	S	S	S	S	S	H	H	H	H*	H
14	S	S	S	S	S	H	H	H	H	H
13	S	S	S	S	S	H	H	H	H	H
12	H	H	S	S	S	H	H	H	H	H
11	D	D	D	D	D	D	D	D	D	H
10	D	D	D	D	D	D	D	D	H	H
A,A	P	P	P	P	P	P	P	P	P	P
10,10	S	S	S	S	S	S	S	S	S	S
9,9	P	P	P	P	P	S	P	P	S	S
8,8	P	P	P	P	P	P	P	P	P	P
7,7	P	P	P	P	P	P	H	H	H	H
6,6	H	P	P	P	P	H	H	H	H	H
5,5		Always Treat as 10, never Split								
4,4	H	H	H	H	H	H	H	H	H	H
3,3	H	H	P	P	P	P	H	H	H	H
2,2	H	H	P	P	P	P	H	H	H	H

*Surrender if offered

S= STAND   H= HIT   D= DOUBLE   P=SPLIT

A,2 through A,6 always *hit*.

A,8 through A,10 always *stand*.

A,7 *hit* on dealer's 9, 10, A and *stand* on 2 through 8.

Chart 4

141

Single Deck Basic Strategy
Dealer stands on soft 17
Doubling on any two cards
Doubling after pair splitting *not* permitted

Dealer's Upcard

Your Hand	2	3	4	5	6	7	8	9	10	A
17	S	S	S	S	S	S	S	S	S	S
16	S	S	S	S	S	H	H	H	H*	H
15	S	S	S	S	S	H	H	H	H*	H
14	S	S	S	S	S	H	H	H	H	H
13	S	S	S	S	S	H	H	H	H	H
12	H	H	S	S	S	H	H	H	H	H
11	D	D	D	D	D	D	D	D	D	D
10	D	D	D	D	D	D	D	D	H	H
9	D	D	D	D	D	H	H	H	H	H
5,3	H	H	H	D	D	H	H	H	H	H
A,8	S	S	S	S	D	S	S	S	S	S
A,7	S	D	D	D	D	S	S	H	H	H
A,6	D	D	D	D	D	H	H	H	H	H
A,5	H	H	D	D	D	H	H	H	H	H
A,4	H	H	D	D	D	H	H	H	H	H
A,3	H	H	D	D	D	H	H	H	H	H
A,2	H	H	D	D	D	H	H	H	H	H
A,A	P	P	P	P	P	P	P	P	P	P
10,10	S	S	S	S	S	S	S	S	S	S
9,9	P	P	P	P	P	S	P	P	S	S
8,8	P	P	P	P	P	P	P	P	P	P
7,7	P	P	P	P	P	P	H	H	S*	H
6,6	P	P	P	P	P	H	H	H	H	H
5,5	Always Treat as 10, never Split									
4,4	H	H	H	D	D	H	H	H	H	H
3,3	H	H	P	P	P	P	H	H	H	H
2,2	H	P	P	P	P	P	H	H	H	H

*Surrender if offered

S= STAND **H= HIT** **D= DOUBLE** **P=SPLIT**

Chart 5

Single Deck Basic Strategy
Dealer stands on soft 17
Doubling on any two cards
Doubling after pair splitting permitted

Your Hand	Dealer's Upcard 2	3	4	5	6	7	8	9	10	A
17	S	S	S	S	S	S	S	S	S	S
16	S	S	S	S	S	H	H	H	H*	H
15	S	S	S	S	S	H	H	H	H*	H
14	S	S	S	S	S	H	H	H	H	H
13	S	S	S	S	S	H	H	H	H	H
12	H	H	S	S	S	H	H	H	H	H
11	D	D	D	D	D	D	D	D	D	D
10	D	D	D	D	D	D	D	D	H	H
9	D	D	D	D	D	H	H	H	H	H
5,3	H	H	H	D	D	H	H	H	H	H
A,8	S	S	S	S	D	S	S	S	S	S
A,7	S	D	D	D	D	S	S	H	H	H
A,6	D	D	D	D	D	H	H	H	H	H
A,5	H	H	D	D	D	H	H	H	H	H
A,4	H	H	D	D	D	H	H	H	H	H
A,3	H	H	D	D	D	H	H	H	H	H
A,2	H	H	D	D	D	H	H	H	H	H
A,A	P	P	P	P	P	P	P	P	P	P
10,10	S	S	S	S	S	S	S	S	S	S
9,9	P	P	P	P	P	S	P	P	S	S
8,8	P	P	P	P	P	P	P	P	P	P
7,7	P	P	P	P	P	P	P	H	S*	H
6,6	P	P	P	P	P	P	H	H	H	H
5,5	Always Treat as 10, never Split									
4,4	H	H	P	P	P	H	H	H	H	H
3,3	P	P	P	P	P	P	H	H	H	H
2,2	P	P	P	P	P	P	H	H	H	H

*Surrender if offered

S= STAND H= HIT D= DOUBLE P=SPLIT

Chart 6   **143**

Single Deck Basic Strategy
Dealer stands on soft 17
Doubling only on 10 and 11
Doubling after pair splitting *not* permitted

Your Hand	2	3	4	5	6	7	8	9	10	A
17	S	S	S	S	S	S	S	S	S	S
16	S	S	S	S	S	H	H	H	H*	H
15	S	S	S	S	S	H	H	H	H*	H
14	S	S	S	S	S	H	H	H	H	H
13	S	S	S	S	S	H	H	H	H	H
12	H	H	S	S	S	H	H	H	H	H
11	D	D	D	D	D	D	D	D	D	D
10	D	D	D	D	D	D	D	D	H	H
A,A	P	P	P	P	P	P	P	P	P	P
10,10	S	S	S	S	S	S	S	S	S	S
9,9	P	P	P	P	P	S	P	P	S	S
8,8	P	P	P	P	P	P	P	P	P	P
7,7	P	P	P	P	P	P	H	H	S*	H
6,6	P	P	P	P	P	H	H	H	H	H
5,5				Always Treat as 10, never split						
4,4	H	H	H	H	H	H	H	H	H	H
3,3	H	H	P	P	P	P	H	H	H	H
2,2	H	P	P	P	P	P	H	H	H	H

Dealer's Upcard

*Surrender if offered
S= STAND   H= HIT   D= DOUBLE   P=SPLIT

A,2 through A,6 always *hit*.
A,8 through A,10 always *stand*.
A,7 *hit* on dealer's 9, 10, A and *stand* on 2 through 8.

Chart 7

Single Deck Basic Strategy
Dealer hits soft 17
Doubling only on 10 and 11
Doubling after pair splitting *not* permitted

Your Hand	Dealer's Upcard									
	2	3	4	5	6	7	8	9	10	A
17	S	S	S	S	S	S	S	S	S	S
16	S	S	S	S	S	H	H	H	H	H
15	S	S	S	S	S	H	H	H	H	H
14	S	S	S	S	S	H	H	H	H	H
13	S	S	S	S	S	H	H	H	H	H
12	H	H	S	S	S	H	H	H	H	H
11	D	D	D	D	D	D	D	D	D	D
10	D	D	D	D	D	D	D	D	H	H
A,A	P	P	P	P	P	P	P	P	P	P
10,10	S	S	S	S	S	S	S	S	S	S
9,9	P	P	P	P	P	S	P	P	S	P
8,8	P	P	P	P	P	P	P	P	P	P
7,7	P	P	P	P	P	P	H	H	S	H
6,6	P	P	P	P	P	H	H	H	H	H
5,5	Always Treat as 10, never Split									
4,4	H	H	H	H	H	H	H	H	H	H
3,3	H	H	P	P	P	P	H	H	H	H
2,2	H	H	P	P	P	P	H	H	H	H

S= STAND   H= HIT   D= DOUBLE   P= SPLIT

A,2 through A,6 always *hit*.

A,8 through A,10 always *stand*.

A,7 *hit* on dealer's 9, 10, A and *stand* on 2 through 8.

Chart 8

Double Deck Basic Strategy
Dealer stands on soft 17
Doubling on any two cards
Doubling after pair splitting *not* permitted

Dealer's Upcard

Your Hand	2	3	4	5	6	7	8	9	10	A
17	S	S	S	S	S	S	S	S	S	S
16	S	S	S	S	S	H	H	H	H*	H*
15	S	S	S	S	S	H	H	H	H*	H
14	S	S	S	S	S	H	H	H	H	H
13	S	S	S	S	S	H	H	H	H	H
12	H	H	S	S	S	H	H	H	H	H
11	D	D	D	D	D	D	D	D	D	H
10	D	D	D	D	D	D	D	D	H	H
9	H	D	D	D	D	H	H	H	H	H
53	H	H	H	H	H	H	H	H	H	H
A,8	S	S	S	S	S	S	S	S	S	S
A,7	S	D	D	D	D	S	S	H	H	H
A,6	H	D	D	D	D	H	H	H	H	H
A,5	H	H	D	D	D	H	H	H	H	H
A,4	H	H	D	D	D	H	H	H	H	H
A,3	H	H	H	D	D	H	H	H	H	H
A,2	H	H	H	D	D	H	H	H	H	H
A,A	P	P	P	P	P	P	P	P	P	P
10,10	S	S	S	S	S	S	S	S	S	S
9,9	P	P	P	P	P	S	P	P	S	S
8,8	P	P	P	P	P	P	P	P	P	P
7,7	P	P	P	P	P	P	H	H	H	H
6,6	P	P	P	P	P	H	H	H	H	H
5,5	Always Treat as 10, never Split									
4,4	H	H	H	H	H	H	H	H	H	H
3,3	H	H	P	P	P	P	H	H	H	H
2,2	H	H	P	P	P	P	H	H	H	H

*Surrender if offered
S= STAND   H= HIT   D= DOUBLE   P=SPLIT

Chart 9

Double Deck Basic Strategy
Dealer stands on soft 17
Doubling on any two cards
Doubling after pair splitting permitted

Your Hand	Dealer's Upcard									
	2	3	4	5	6	7	8	9	10	A
17	S	S	S	S	S	S	S	S	S	S
16	S	S	S	S	S	H	H	H	H*	H*
15	S	S	S	S	S	H	H	H	H*	H
14	S	S	S	S	S	H	H	H	H	H
13	S	S	S	S	S	H	H	H	H	H
12	H	H	S	S	S	H	H	H	H	H
11	D	D	D	D	D	D	D	D	D	H
10	D	D	D	D	D	D	D	D	H	H
9	D	D	D	D	D	H	H	H	H	H
53	H	H	H	H	H	H	H	H	H	H
A,8	S	S	S	S	S	S	S	S	S	S
A,7	S	D	D	D	D	S	S	H	H	H
A,6	H	D	D	D	D	H	H	H	H	H
A,5	H	H	D	D	D	H	H	H	H	H
A,4	H	H	D	D	D	H	H	H	H	H
A,3	H	H	H	D	D	H	H	H	H	H
A,2	H	H	H	D	D	H	H	H	H	H
A,A	P	P	P	P	P	P	P	P	P	P
10,10	S	S	S	S	S	S	S	S	S	S
9,9	P	P	P	P	P	S	P	P	S	S
8,8	P	P	P	P	P	P	P	P	P	P
7,7	P	P	P	P	P	P	H	H	H	H
6,6	P	P	P	P	P	H	H	H	H	H
5,5	Always Treat as 10, never Split									
4,4	H	H	H	P	P	H	H	H	H	H
3,3	P	P	P	P	P	P	H	H	H	H
2,2	P	P	P	P	P	P	H	H	H	H

*Surrender if offered
S= STAND   H= HIT   D= DOUBLE   P=SPLIT

Chart 10   147

Basic Strategy for Six (6) Deck Spanish 21[1]

Player	2	3	4	5	6	7	8	9	10	A
21	S	S	S	S	S	S	S	S	S	S
20	S	S	S	S	S	S	S	S	S	S
19	S	S	S	S	S	S	S	S	S	S
18	S	S	S	S	S	S	S	S	S	S
17	S	S	S	S	S	S	H6	H6	H6	SR
16	H5	H6	H6	S	S	H	H	H	H	SR
15	H4	H5	H5	H6	H6	H	H	H	H	H
14	H	H	H4	H5	H5	H	H	H	H	H
13	H	H	H	H	H4	H	H	H	H	H
12	H	H	H	H	H	H	H	H	H	H
11	4DB	5DB	5DB	5BD	5DB	4DB	4DB	H	H	H
10	5DB	5DB	6DB	D	D	4DB	H	H	H	H
9	H	H	H	H	3DB	H	H	H	H	H
8	H	H	H	H	H	H	H	H	H	H
7	H	H	H	H	H	H	H	H	H	H
6	H	H	H	H	H	H	H	H	H	H
5	H	H	H	H	H	H	H	H	H	H
4	H	H	H	H	H	H	H	H	H	H
SOFT 21	H	H	H	H	H	H	H	H	H	H
SOFT 20	H	H	H	H	H	H	H	H	H	H
SOFT 19	H	H	H	H	H	H	H	H	H	H
SOFT 18	H4	H4	4DB	5DB	6DB	S	H4	H	H	H
SOFT 17	H	H	3DB	4DB	5DB	H	H	H	H	H
SOFT 16	H	H	H	H	4DB	H	H	H	H	H
SOFT 15	H	H	H	H	H	H	H	H	H	H
SOFT 14	H	H	H	H	H	H	H	H	H	H
SOFT 13	H	H	H	H	H	H	H	H	H	H
PAIR A	P	P	P	P	P	P	P	P	P	P
PAIR 10	S	S	S	S	S	S	S	S	S	S
PAIR 9	S	P	P	P	P	S	P	P	S	S
PAIR 8	P	P	P	P	P	P	P	P	P	SR
PAIR 7	P	P	P	P	P	*P	H	H	H	H
PAIR 6	H	H	P	P	P	H	H	H	H	H
PAIR 5	D	D	D	D	D	D	H	H	H	H
PAIR 4	H	H	H	H	H	H	H	H	H	H
PAIR 3	H	P	P	P	P	P	H	H	H	H
PAIR 2	H	P	P	P	P	P	H	H	H	H

*Pair of same color 7s (suited) against Dealer 7, hit.
S = Stand   D = Double   H = Hit   P = Split   SR = Surrender
H4, (H5, H6) = hit hands of 4 (5, 6) or more cards, else stand
3DB, 4DB, 5DB, 6DB = HIT 3, 4, 5, 6 or more cards, else double
[1]*Strategy obtained from Kinetic Gaming Group*

APPENDIX II

Summary of Crap Bets

Bet	Casino Advantage (%)
Pass Line	1.41
Don't Pass Line	1.40
Come	1.41
Don't Come	1.40
Place 6 and 8 to win	1.51
Place 5 and 9 to win	4.00
Place 4 and 10 to win	6.67
Buy 6 or 8	4.76
Buy 5 or 9	4.76
Buy 4 or 10	4.76
Lay 6 or 8	4.00
Lay 5 or 9	3.23
Lay 4 or 10	2.44
Field	5.56
Big 6 or 8	9.09
Any Craps	11.11
Hardway 6 or 8	9.09
Hardway 4 or 10	11.10
11 or 3 Proposition	11.10
2 or 12 Proposition	13.90
Any Seven	16.70

INDEX

PUBLICATIONS BY HENRY J. TAMBURIN

Blackjack: Take the Money and Run

Win at blackjack! This book will teach you how to walk away from the blackjack tables with profits. The winning techniques are based on Dr. Tamburin's 27 years of experience as a winning blackjack player. You'll learn the basics of how the game is played and which blackjack games offer you the most profit potential, a non-counting winning strategy for the beginner, a unique streak count betting system for the intermediate player, and a powerful advanced level system that will give you up to a 1.5% edge over the casinos. The ultimate source of blackjack winning techniques for all players who want to improve their game. $15.00

Blackjack - Deal Me In Video

Play like an expert after you view this video! Filmed in a Mississippi casino with a professional dealer, Henry Tamburin will guide you with clear explanations and demonstrations on how to play blackjack, the different rules and playing options, the basic playing strategy, and how to manage your money for maximum profits. After viewing this tape you'll know how to pick a table, how to use hand signals, how to keep more of your winnings, and when to move to another table. You'll know *exactly* when to take a hit, when to stand, when to double down, which pairs to split, and how to tip the dealer. This professionally produced, 90 minute, full color VHS video also contains graphics that highlight the strategies and a handy index that allows fast forwarding to review any topic. Makes learning how to play and win at blackjack fun and easy. $34.95

Craps: Take the Money and Run

Win at craps! This book will teach you how to walk away from the tables with profits. You'll learn the basics of the game including an explanation of all the different types of bets on the layout. More importantly, you'll learn Dr. Tamburin's increased odds playing system that will allow you to cut the casino's edge to less than 1% and cash in on a hot roll. $15.00

Craps - Rolling To Win Video

Play like an expert after you view this video! Filmed in a Mississippi casino with professional dealers, this video will guide you with clear explanations and demonstrations how to play craps with playing tips to improve your chances of winning. You will be able to play like a pro after viewing this video! Professionally produced, 90 minutes, full color video with graphics makes learning how to play and win at craps fun and easy. $34.95

Reference Guide to Casino Gambling Second Edition

This book contains the basic playing rules and winning tips for 25 of the most popular casino games offered in land and water based casinos throughout the country. Includes blackjack, craps, roulette, baccarat, video poker, big six wheel, pai gow poker, Caribbean stud, slots, keno, sic bo, lowball, red dog, hold'em, draw poker, seven card stud, Spanish 21, heads up blackjack, live video blackjack, live video craps, progressive blackjack, never ever craps, crap shoot, and multiple action blackjack. $15.00

The Ten Best Casino Bets Second Edition

A pocket size book that explains how to make the ten most player favorable bets in a casino. Includes blackjack, craps pass/don't pass with odds, baccarat bank and player bets, craps place bets on 6 and 8, video poker, craps lay bet on 4 and 10, pai gow poker, and roulette. Also contains chapters on betting strategies, money management, and the psychology of gambling. Great book for the novice to intermediate player. $5.00

Winning Baccarat Strategies

This classic book contains effective card counting systems for the casino game of baccarat. You'll learn how the game is played, a simple running count system, the true count system, how to put the count to work, money management concepts, and ESP and baccarat. The counting strategies are based on three years of intensive research and the computer analysis of more than *175 million games*. Even if you've never played baccarat, this book will quickly teach you the strategies and techniques for winning play. $20.00

Pocket Blackjack Strategy Card

A durable, plastic coated, hand held pocket card that contains the complete blackjack playing strategy. Take it with you to the tables and refer to it. You will never make a costly playing mistake! Casino legal. Makes *any* player a *skillful* player. $3.00

To order any of the above, send name and address with check or money order to:

Research Services Unlimited
P.O. Box 19727
Greensboro, NC 27419
(The above prices include shipping and handling)

About the Author

Henry Tamburin has been actively involved in casino gambling for the past 27 years as a player, author, instructor, and columnist. He has operated a casino gambling school to teach winning techniques to the public, written and published a newsletter on Atlantic City casino gambling and operated a club for casino players. He has written over 500 articles on casino gambling that have appeared in every major gaming magazine. His "how to win" seminars are well received by clubs/organizations. Henry has appeared on TV and radio and his exploits as a winning casino player and public educator have been featured in several newspaper stories. Most recently he is featured in the new instructional videos *Blackjack - Deal Me In* and *Craps - Rolling To Win*.

His books include: *Blackjack: Take the Money and Run, Craps: Take the Money and Run, Reference Guide to Casino Gambling Second Edition, The Ten Best Casino Bets Second Edition, Winning Baccarat Strategies, WBS Chart Book, Henry Tamburin on Casino Gambling, Casino Gambler's Survival Book, Casino Gambler's Quiz Book,* and *Pocket Guide to Casino Gambling.*

Henry Tamburin is a graduate of Seton Hall University with a Bachelor of Science degree in Chemistry, and the University of Maryland with a Doctor of Philosophy degree in Organic Chemistry. He works for a large international chemical company. He and his wife Linda have two grown sons.

NOTES

NOTES

NOTES